LIVE AS LONG AS YOU CAN, BUT DON'T GROW OLD

A Man's Quest
On How to Stay Young
All Of Your Life

By

V. Henry Chadwick

LIVE AS LONG AS YOU CAN,
BUT DON'T GROW OLD

A Man's Quest
On How to Stay Young
All Of Your Life

By: V. Henry Chadwick

Copyright ©   2014 by V. Henry Chadwick

ISBN-1502756455
EAN - 9781502756459

This book is dedicated to
Drew, Julia, Swayze, Ian, Price, Lydia,
and my grandchildren,
and to my friends who assisted
in its creation,
Helen, Rob, Sarah Ann, Bob, Mary, and John

TABLE OF CONTENTS

CHAPTER 1

MY QUEST

"Knowledge is of two kinds.
We know a subject ourselves,
or we know where we can find information upon it."
Boswell

"Some day you'll be old like me." It's been over forty years since my father spoke those words to me. He was only sixty years old at the time. Not long afterwards, he quit working, stayed at home, and basically did nothing. He did not read; he had no hobbies; he did not exercise. He would just sit and mosey around the house and yard. Soon, he spent much of his time in bed. Before long, he was totally bedridden. In the end, he only longed for death. His wish was granted when he was only sixty-three years of age.

My father's health was not the best, but, in my opinion, it was not the worst either. His mind was good up until the end, but it wasn't used. His father had lived well into his seventies when he died, and my father's siblings lived well into their eighties; thus heredity should not have been a factor in his early death. I believed then, as I do now, that my father just gave up on life. I have no doubt that he could have kept on working if he had so desired, pursuing new dreams and goals, and continued to be a productive citizen and active family member for many more years; but, instead, he abandoned life and grew old.

I had come back to my hometown to practice law with my father four years before his pronouncement, never realizing that he would end his life that way. But as his life unraveled and his intentions became clear that he would never return to the office, at age thirty, I shut down the office, closed out my practice, and left our small town to start my life over again. But those seven words spoken by my father and the way he lived until he died never left my mind. It's as if those words were seared like a cattle brand on the back of my brain.

Since my father's death, I have witnessed many others who have taken the same path — choosing to forsake life and calling on death long before it should come. They, like my father, lost all zest for life, and fell into the doldrums until the angel of death arrived.

Yet, on the other hand, I have witnessed those in bad health, even with severe disabilities, who did not give up on life, but who kept a youthfulness about them as they grew older and continued to live life to its fullest until their time came. Why is it that some, like my father, grew old before their time, while others appeared to stay young throughout their entire lives? What was it that allowed many to have long lives, but more importantly, what was it that gave them a gusto for life throughout their lives even though the calendar said they were old? What is it about some people that allows them to continue to enjoy life, pursue dreams, and remain happy right up until their deaths, while others merely live an existence that slowly drowns them in self-pity until they are rescued by death?

Ever since my father's death, I have continued to ponder this phenomenon, and these questions have continued to perplex me all through the years. I knew as I grew older that I did not want to be like my father and the many others who gave up on life. I wanted to live a long life, and hopefully, a rewarding one, especially in my latter years. But I had no answers to these questions.

However, in 1997 all of this would change. I was fifty-six years old, my family and I were in New York City for the Thanksgiving holidays. Macy's Parade was finally winding down. So was I. The weather was brutally cold that day, the wintry wind was piercing through my thick coat, and my nose felt as if it had turned to ice. I was beginning to feel puny so I sought refuge from the elements in our warm and cozy hotel room. In an attempt to guard against any ailment that might be coming (real or imagined), I made two requests of my family as I crawled under the covers of the bed.

One, that someone bring me a bowl of Matzoh Ball soup from the Carnegie Deli, and two, the latest edition of the *New York Times*. Fortunately, the Deli was across the street, and a newsstand was close by. Even though the soup came in a styrofoam-like bowl with a plastic spoon, it perked up my spirits as I slurped the hot broth and skimmed the news. Working through the many pages of print, I reached the obituary section. It was there that my eyes caught a notice of the death of a 101 year old lady, Hulda Crooks. As I read, I was spellbound. Hulda Crooks had climbed twenty-three times to the top of Mt. Whitney, the tallest mountain peak in the continental United States. But what was amazing was that her first climb was in her sixties when most people believe they are too old for such an endeavor. And even more amazing was that her last climb to the top of that vast mountain was twenty-five years later when she was over ninety. As I read about this unbelievable and fascinating woman, it became clear to me that no one should give up because they have gotten older. She demonstrated to me that feats and accomplishments can be attained at all ages. I was so taken aback by her life that I knew I could no longer just ponder the questions surrounding my father's statement and subsequent death, and that I must do something to find the answers to my questions. What is it that Hulda Crooks had that my father didn't? Why is it that he would die "an old man" at age sixty-three, and she would die "young" at 101? I realized that to find the answers to these questions I must research in depth every source available to me. So I set to work.

I first contacted Ms. Crooks' family in California and learned that she had written a book about her life entitled *Conquering Life's Mountains*. I also learned that another book had been written about her life entitled *Grandma Whitney Queen of the Mountain*. I immediately ordered the two books. Several days later when the postman delivered them to my office, I stopped everything and began to read.

Ms. Crooks was born in 1896 in Saskatchewan, Canada, the fifth child of the family. She would grow up in Canada, and at a young age, marry Sam Crooks, a fellow Canadian. In time, Hulda and Sam moved from Canada to Loma Linda, California where they would reside for the rest of their lives. Unfortunately, Hulda became a widow at age fifty-four; however, she did not stop living as a result of her husband's death. Instead, she took up mountain-climbing. At age sixty-six, she would climb Mt. Whitney which stands 14,495 feet tall. It would be her first time to climb this massive mountain. In addition to mountain climbing, she also began hiking. At age seventy-six, she hiked eighty miles across the Sierra Nevada Mountain Range. At age seventy-seven, she made another ninety-six mile hike. Even though she was now hiking, she continued her mountain climbing, and at seventy-eight, Hulda climbed Mt. Whitney for the thirteenth time. She never tired of her mountain climbing or of Mt. Whitney. At age eighty-four, she would climb Mt. Whitney again — for the nineteenth time. At eighty-six, she would make a forty mile backpack trip through the Cottonwood Pass in the Rocky Mountain Range in Colorado. Afterwards, at eighty-nine, she would once again climb Mt. Whitney, becoming the oldest person to do so.

However, there was another mountain that challenged her — Mt. Fuji in Japan. She would climb Mt. Fuji at age ninety-one, becoming the oldest woman to ever climb that mountain. Astonishingly, six weeks after her Mt. Fuji climb, she would make her last climb of Mt. Whitney. This short, petite, gray-haired, blue-eyed lady, with her soft sole shoes and her tall walking stick, climbed Mt. Whitney for the twenty-third time at age ninety-one. She was so revered for love of mountain climbing and for her love of Mt. Whitney, she would be forever known as "Grandma Whitney". Even a peak on Mt. Whitney at 14,240 feet has been named "Crooks Peak" in her honor. And a park in her beloved city of Loma Linda was also named in her honor, "Hulda Crooks Park".

After finishing the books about Ms. Crooks, I was eager to find other people like her that seemingly had the spirit that I was looking for. I first delved into my home library and began reading an old, worn-out *Funk & Wagnalls* encyclopedia set that my wife had inherited from her parents. It was informative, but it only gave me snippets of lives and information on people rather than detailed information about their lives, but it was sufficient to give me a starting point from which to work. You might think that reading an encyclopedia would be a monotonous and laborious task, but, in actuality, I found it very entertaining, and I learned a lot. In my free time from work, I would flip through the pages, with my project in mind, searching for people, particularly beyond the age of sixty who might be a candidate for my quest. If there were none who interested me, I would keep moving through the pages. However, any that did interest me, I would make a note for future study. Trying to focus mainly only on people, I would skip through the sections that dealt with insects, animals, countries, and other minutiae; but, if something interesting did catch my eye, I would stop and read whether it pertained to my project or not. However, any other subjects that I did feel were important for my project, such as health, medicine, aging, longevity, or unusual feats, I would make note of it as I did with people. This task took many weeks. But, before long, I realized that I had completed the entire encyclopedia set which covered thirty-six volumes and 13,530 pages.

After finishing *Funk & Wagnalls,* I then began reading and studying *The Story of Civilization* by Will and Ariel Durant. The Durants' history consists of eleven volumes covering the beginning of civilization up to the 19th century. It was more comprehensive than the encyclopedia and more interesting as well, but it was a much slower process. More details were given regarding peoples' lives, such as physical descriptions, health problems, personalties, highs and lows in their lives, and how they may have handled life in general. While I was reading *The Story of Civilization,* I also began a daily task of reading obituary columns, along with other newspaper articles that might reveal answers to my query. My objective was to find any article, obituary, or other information that could assist me. If I found a person or something that might aid me, I would cut out the article or make a copy and place it in a notebook. I also began studying almanacs, reference books, quote books, and dictionaries. In addition, I made constant use of the computer for my research, particularly web-sites such as *The New York Times, Wikipedia,* and *Project Gutenberg.* Also, I made it a point to observe those around me who had reached their senior years to see how they lived. Fortunately, my profession as an attorney which involves elder law has allowed me to work with older people, giving me insight into personality differences and how certain individuals have handled the aging process. I also took time to reflect throughout my own life and how others whom I had known had lived and died.

After completing the Durants' history, to keep moving

forward, I began reading biographies of individuals whom I had made note of so that I could get a complete detailed picture of a life that interested me. Also in my research, I turned to the sages that history deems wise, such as Aristotle, Socrates, and Seneca. Moreover, I made it a point to find people who had lived extra-ordinary lives in hopes of finding their secrets which helped them attain their longevity. I then studied the philosophers such as Immanuel Kant, Schopenhauer, and Rousseau. Also I studied inspiring writers such as James Allen and Emerson; statesmen like Washington, Jefferson, Adams, and Franklin; activists, such as Dorothea Dix and Elizabeth Cady Stanton; and even military figures like Winfield Scott. In addition, I read books on health, happiness, and longevity, and I studied some people who did not have a long life; for instance, Thoreau, who died early in life, but was wise as if he had lived a long life.

I always felt it necessary to delve into the history of all of my subjects for I never felt I could completely understand a subject unless I inquired into its past; thus, I was pleased to learn that the word "history" comes from the Greek language meaning "inquiry". This study of the past led me to other people and subjects that I may not have found otherwise. For instance, my study of history would acquaint me with Marcus Tullius Cicero, who lived at the time of Julius Caesar in ancient Rome. I learned that when Cicero was sixty-two years old, suffering from the recent death of his beloved daughter, Tullia, he retreated to the countryside and wrote a book on old age named *Cato Maior de Senectute* which has been studied down through the ages, becoming an inspiration for many and certainly an inspiration for my own quest.

Often one book, article, or essay would lead me to another. An example of this was when I read James Michener's autobiography, I became aware of Kenneth

Roberts, the author of such books as *Arundel* and *Northwest Passage*. I then read Roberts' autobiographical book, *I Wanted to Write*, but, I did not find much in his life that held my interest; however, I did discover another author, Booth Tarkington, who was a friend and neighbor of Roberts in Maine, who, in his sixties, went blind, yet kept an incredible positive attitude and continued to write until his death at seventy-six by dictating to his secretary. Also, when I read the biography of John D. Rockefeller, Sr., I learned of a lady with a strange name of Ida Tarbell, who was a journalist during the time of the "muckrakers". Her reporting and her coverage of Rockefeller and his oil empire would be a major factor in dismantling his empire, for it was deemed a monopoly arising out of the so-called "Robber Baron Days". She would intrigue me. This lady lived a most active and fruitful life, writing her autobiography in her eighties with the attitude and energy of a thirty year old. She was the type of person I was looking for. She made me realize that I needed to continue for I wanted to discover more like her.

However, even though I was progressing, at times I felt like I was on a long treasure hunt, but with no map. But my method was working. Thus I continued my quest which would ultimately result in reading more than two hundred biographies, plus numerous articles, essays, and the like. Also, my readings and studies resulted in a collection of newspaper articles, information downloaded from the internet, and written notes of my own — all of which grew into fifteen volumes of notebooks filled with data.

Moreover, in my search, I decided not to judge anyone regarding their political agenda or their religion since my purpose was to study those who maintained a youthful attitude throughout their lives — regardless of their beliefs. I was only looking for people who lived their lives, particularly in their latter years, who dealt with the aging process as if they had discovered "the fountain of youth". I wanted to find people who continued to grow all of their lives, who found real meaning in their lives, and who led full and happy lives, even if they suffered difficulties, whether physical, financial, or otherwise, and how they dealt with those problems, and not let their political or religious beliefs affect my undertaking.

During the period of my research, I continued to pursue a career and live a full life. After a day at the office, I would read, study, or plow through my material in search of my objective. While others were watching *Law & Order*, I was reading Montaigne. Even though I started over fourteen years ago, I tried to stay on course; but I have to confess at times I got off track. The demands of my profession caused delays, and sometimes, I just wanted to take a break and read a detective novel, rather than research. However, regardless of these breaks in the chain, I would always return with new vigor and interest in my pursuit. When I learned that Johann Wolfgang von Goethe had worked on writing his masterpiece *Faust* on and off for over fifty years and yet did not finish until he was eighty-one years old, I felt better about my pauses from my project and the time it was taking me to finish my goal.

Regardless of the years spent in my pursuit, my time has not been wasted for I have learned, and it is clear to me, that most of us can live long lives and not grow old like my father did. As a result of my findings, I am convinced that nursing homes and elder care facilities which are full, need not be, and even though there may be problems in one's life, that this is a part of living, and should not be a reason to give up. I am further convinced that anyone, regardless of their age, health, financial condition, or any other impediment, can still continue to achieve goals and live a full and productive life throughout their whole lives.

After I had been working on my project for several years, an elderly gentleman came to my office. We talked briefly about the weather and life in general, and then he made a statement that summed up what my project was all about. He said, "Live as long as you can, but don't grow old."

This book is about what I found and what I've learned from my quest.

CHAPTER 2

THE PAIN AND PLEASURES OF AGING

"Make me lame in hand
Lame in foot and thigh
Shake out my loosened teeth;
while life stays, so stay I."
Maecenas

It is pretty universal that most of us want to live a long life, but one of the most important lessons that I have learned is that if you want to live a long life, you must accept the consequences of aging. While every stage of life has its problems, aging's problems lie in the slow decline of our bodies. My wife's father, who lived into his nineties, said that aging is not for sissies. I agree. There is no doubt that there is a price to be paid for longevity.

Sir John Lubbock, who wrote *The Pleasures of Life* in the 19th century, said, "When we consider the marvelous complexity of our bodily organization, it seems a miracle that we should live at all; much more that the innumerable organs and processes should continue day after day and year after year with so much regularity and so little friction that we are sometimes scarcely conscious of having a body at all." The comments of Lubbock are certainly true; however, I have found that if you live long enough, you will become conscious of your body and its limitations.

Your body is like an automobile; as you drive it each day, it slowly wears out. By the time you are sixty, you've probably blinked 460 million times, breathed 350 million times, eaten 66,000 meals, your heart has beaten 2.2 billion times, you've slept 175,000 hours, produced 15,000 gallons of urine, and taken 132 million steps. Compared to that automobile, at sixty, your body has reached 100,000 miles. If you are lucky enough to reach 100 years, you will have blinked 700 million times, breathed 580 million times, eaten 110,000 meals which would have required your digestive system to have processed enough food to fill as many as thirty railroad cars, your heart will have beaten 3.7 billion times, you will have slept 292,000 hours, produced 25,000 gallons of urine, and taken 230 million steps. Amazingly, your body now, like that automobile, has reached 300,000 miles. You may have replaced joints like you replaced the tires on your automobile, and taken your vitamins like you changed your automobile's oil, and if you've taken care of your body by following the regimens set by doctors and health gurus regarding diet, exercise, and medicine, you may fare better than others, but you still will not avoid the consequences of aging. So by the time you reach that milestone of 100, your body is in the same condition as that old automobile, and both are probably ready for the junkyard.

You cannot escape the aging process. As Shakespeare said, "we ripe and ripe and then we rot and rot and therein lies the tale." The ancient Roman statesman Cicero described it further and said, "...just as to the berries of a tree and the fruits of the earth there comes in the fullness of time ... a period of decay and fall." At first, the aging process was in a positive manner until you reached about eighteen; but, then the aging process turned from positive to negative. Your strength and probably your coordination peaked at nineteen. Your stamina may have peaked at about age thirty. By age forty, in all likelihood, you may have noticed changes in your body such as graying hair, wrinkles, less strength, less speed, higher blood pressure, liver spots, hearing loss, diminished eyesight, and more than likely you started losing more bone than you were making. By age fifty, your skin began getting thinner, things started popping up on your skin as if you were an old gnarled tree, your hands began to show your veins more readily, the veins seemed to be darker, and your face and neck began to sag. A face lift may give the appearance that you are younger, but the backs of your hands will still reveal your secret; and on the inside, your organs and other parts of your body will still continue to age. You may not have noticed it, but by age sixty, probably your arteries began to clog, and your body doesn't function as it used to, so you most likely had to start taking pills which may continue to increase as you get older. In fact, Dr. Seuss, the children's book writer, who produced such books as *The Cat in the Hat,* became so enthralled with aging that he wrote a "children's book for adults" describing the effects of getting older and the pills you may have to take and named the book aptly, *You're Only Old Once.* Also there may be other changes as we age. For instance, you may lose hair where you want it the most, but begin to grow hair where you want it the least. And my wife of fifty years says that I've begun to mumble to myself (which may be true) but she has begun to snore – quite loudly I may add.

Even though we all continue to age as long as we live, some of us refuse to see it in ourselves. For example, I met a man when I was stationed in the military in the Philippine Islands who tried to convince me that he had not aged as others had. He said that he had been living in the Philippines for a number of years, and as a result of the tropical weather, he had a perpetual oil on his skin which prevented the aging process from taking place as it would in a cooler climate such as the United States. After expounding on his theory, he then asked me to guess how old he was. I took a minute and assessed his appearance. He was slightly stooped, wrinkled, balding, and had an ashen complexion. Trying to be honest, I told him he looked about seventy to me. With that, his face turned red, he got mad, told me he was in his fifties, and then abruptly left.

The gentleman from the Philippines obviously could not see the aging of his own body, whereas, I could see that he had aged. Another example of recognizing aging in others, but not necessarily in ourselves, is seeing an old friend after a long absence. I am amazed at how they have changed, and they probably think the same about me. But, like the gentleman from the Philippines, when I look in the mirror, I rarely see the changes in myself.

Aging affects all of us. We watch sexy starlets turn into flabby matrons, and, of course, some of the young hunks turn into fat slobs in their elder years. In fact, some age in such a manner that they aren't even recognizable in their latter years. And who would ever have thought that the Beatles would age when they were asking in their song, "will you still feed me when I'm sixty-four?"

The aging process can be gruesome, and obviously aging does have its problems, but, they may not be as bad as they appear, for Bob Hope once said, "The hardest thing about being ninety years old is answering all the questions about being ninety years old." And even though there may be problems, I can assure you that aging also has its pleasures. Getting older is not all doom and gloom. There can be positive aspects as well. In fact, when you've reached the age of sixty, your hair may have grayed, but, your brain has stored at least four times the information than it contained at age twenty-one; thus, you should be wiser, which can off-set that gray hair.

In fact, there have been studies which show that the brain has a way of compensating as we age, which I believe keeps us wise. It seems that the brain retains its capacity to form new memories and can grow new brain cells as we age. Also, the older person can use both sides of their brain at the same time, whereas, those younger may only use one side at a time; thus, if we exercise our brains, we should keep mentally alert, regardless of how old we may be.

Moreover, an older brain may be as good as or better than a younger brain in many cases. So, as we age, we should be better able to handle the demands we encounter in life and retain competitiveness. I believe this is why older professionals can hold their own against their younger competitors, such as William Gladstone, who was running England as Prime Minister in his eighties and maintaining his hobby of felling trees, and Roger Taney, who was appointed United States Supreme Court Justice by Andrew Jackson who was still serving at age eighty-six when Abraham Lincoln was president. In fact, in 1202, Doge Enrico Dandolo was in charge of Venice at the age of ninety-four, and in his ninety-fifth year, he commanded the Venetian fleet, capturing Constantinople. Dandolo did all of this even after he had lost most of his sight.

Even in ancient times, it was recognized that the elders of the community had to be called on to save a government from the mistakes of the young. While the young may have had energy, the elders had wisdom. Cicero addressed this very situation when he stated that in " ... history you will find that the mightiest states have been brought into peril by younger men and have been supported and restored by the old." In fact, Cicero reminds us that the elders of society have been the mainstay throughout the years and "that sound sense only comes with advancing years." A good example of elders coming to the rescue in ancient times was when the Roman statesman, Appius Claudius, although blind and over ninety, stopped the Roman Senate from making a major mistake by proposing peace with Pyrrhus, the Greek king, who had defeated the Romans in battle. Claudius was led into the Senate where he reminded the young members that, "Rome never makes terms of peace with a victorious enemy on Italian soil." This action by Claudius would result in the Romans continuing to fight for Rome until the Greeks withdrew.

Also, the philosopher, Arthur Schopenhauer, reflected on aging and how the elder can even be mentally superior to the younger at times. He said that it is only when a person gets older that he can be "really rich in experience or in learning" for the elder has had "time and opportunity enough to enable him to see and think over life from all its sides." Schopenhauer further assures us that "in old age there comes an increased depth in the knowledge that was acquired in youth" and that "things which [the elder] thought he knew when he was young, he now knows in reality." He went on to say that the elder's "range of knowledge is wider and in whatever direction it extends, it is thorough, and therefore formed into a consistent and connected whole; whereas in youth knowledge is always defective and fragmentary." All of this points to the fact that the older we become, the wiser we become.

In addition to attaining wisdom as we age, another positive is that we still retain our creativity. It doesn't diminish. It appears that creativity can be found at any age, and that the elder may be even more creative because of a greater knowledge and experience. For example, Plato was still writing at eighty, Verdi composed the opera *Falstaff* at age eighty, and Renaissance artist Titian, with his fading blue eyes, white hair, and trembling hands, was still painting masterpieces in his nineties and would enter into an agreement in 1576 at the age of ninety-nine to paint *Burial of Christ* for the Church of the Frari in Venice.

Actually, the latter part of our life may be the best part of our life, regardless of what the aging process may bring. According to Sir John Sinclair in his book *Code of Health and*

Longevity, old age may be the only period of life in which a person may be properly said to live. He further alluded to the fact that it excels all other periods in understanding and prudence. I share this view for there is a difference between growing older and becoming old. Aging may bring its problems, but that doesn't mean you have to become old. The author Henry Van Dyke chimed in on this very subject when he said, "I shall grow old, but never lose life's zest because the road's last turn will be the best." Others throughout the years have addressed the subject of aging as well. The writer, Jonathan Swift, said that, "no wise man ever wished to be younger." Like Swift, I myself have no desire to be at those younger stages of life which had so many trials and tribulations. Cicero comments on this too – "The course of life is fixed, and nature admits of its being run but one way, and only once; and to each part of our life there is something specially seasonable; so that the feebleness of children, as well as the high spirit of youth, the soberness of maturer years, and the ripe wisdom of old age – all have a certain natural advantage which should be secured in its proper season." Also, we must never forget the words of the poet Robert Browning, "Grow old with me, the best is yet to be. The last of life, for which the first was made."

To further this point, the poet Stanley Kunitz, who entered into a contract agreeing to write three books at the age of eighty-seven, won the National Book Award at age ninety and was appointed America's Poet Laureate at the age of ninety-five, speaking of aging, its problems, and its pleasures. Kunitz, who sported a mustache, thin gray hair, and sad eyes, said, "I don't wake up as a nonagenarian. I wake up as a poet, ... It's only the body that wears out. The imagination is just as intense and glowing as ever... I can scarcely wait till tomorrow. When a new life begins for me, as it does each day... I realize that there are physical penalties that one pays for a long existence... but I am happy to pay

25

them."

I agree with Kunitz in his description about aging. But to have that spirit that he had, it must be remembered that as we get older, we must also get wiser about aging. If we do that, wisdom will teach us that although there are many problems with getting older – just as there were problems when we were younger – there will also be many pleasures as well. In fact, the pleasures should be more. The ancient Greek philosopher Epicurus instructs us that, "as long as we are on the road of life, we must make the latter journey better than the beginning, but be happy and content when we reach the end."

Also among the ancients, the Roman philosopher, Seneca, said that old age should be welcomed, that it is full of pleasure if we so desire. Seneca also tells us that fruit is best at the end of the season, and that every pleasure is most agreeable in the last scene. In more modern times, author W. Somerset Maugham, apparently agreed with the philosophy of Seneca when he wrote, "for the complete life, the perfect pattern, includes old age as well as youth and maturity. The beauty of the morning and radiance of noon are good, but it would be a silly person who drew the curtains and turned out the light in order to shut out the tranquility of evening. Old age has its pleasures, which, though different, are not less than the pleasures of youth." Also, Maugham tells us that there can be many advantages to aging when he wrote "Old age is ready to undertake tasks youth shirked because they would take too long." Maugham is right, for how many times have we seen youth wasted upon the young?

As Maugham reminds us, old age has its pleasures, although they may be different from those of youth. For instance, one of those pleasures is reliving some of the wonderful memories stored in our minds. Nothing is more

pleasing to me than to recall the happy days of my youth and the pleasures that I've had with my family throughout the years. Also among the pleasures which can be enjoyed at any age is seeing a rainbow when its spreads its colorful arch across the sky or a painted butterfly in flight. In fact, Sir John Lubbock teaches us that, "All those who love Nature she loves in return, and will richly reward, not perhaps with the good things, as they are commonly called, but with the best things, of this world; not with money and titles, horses and carriages, but with bright and happy thoughts, contentment and peace of mind... he who loves Nature is always young."

Also no matter how old we may become, we should still be able to enjoy a good movie, read an interesting book, listen to beautiful music, enjoy the birds when they sing, rejoice at the first signs of spring, praise the rays of the sun in summer, awe at the turning of the leaves in the fall, sit by a warm crackling fire in winter, learn something new, listen to the rain on a tin roof, take an afternoon nap, see a falling star, smell the aroma of coffee, hear the honking geese, watch an exciting game, have breakfast for supper on a cold winter night, take a walk in the woods, thrill at the sight of a fishing cork being pulled under, watch the first lightning bug of summer, visit an old friend, witness a flower in bloom, see a pretty girl, enjoy Friday evenings, and feel the love of a cat or dog.

Aside from these pleasures, for many of us, the pleasure of having grandchildren is wonderful because we do not necessarily have the responsibilities designated to their parents. And it has been pointed out that we must not forget that we can also get pleasure from senior discounts on everything from clothes to movies. Also, after sixty you don't have to worry about dying young anymore. And reading the obituary notices in the morning and not finding your name is a pleasure in itself. George Burns, the comedian, said it this

way: "It's nice to be here, when you're ninety-nine years old, it's nice to be anywhere."

Unfortunately, many people fail to recognize and enjoy these pleasures; thus, they fail to age gracefully because they cannot see the advantages of getting older and the pleasures that can still be had along the way. This is what Cicero meant when he said, "Men, of course, who have no resources in themselves for securing a good and happy life find every age burdensome." And this is why I believe it is important to search for those resources that Cicero speaks of in order to enjoy the pleasures of life as we age. So to age gracefully and to enjoy the pleasures, one must mentally prepare for every stage of life, especially the latter stage. I once read that "the world is a beautiful book, but of little use to him who cannot read it." And among the benefits of aging, we must never forget Einstein's statement when he said, "I reached an age when, if someone tells me to wear socks, I don't have to."

CHAPTER 3

LONGEVITY — HOW LONG CAN YOU LIVE?

"The horse and the mule live 30 years
And know nothing of wine and beers,
The cow drinks water by the ton
And at 18 is nearly done.
The dog at 15 cashes in
Without the aid of rum or gin.
The cat in milk and water soaks
And then at 12 short years it croaks.
The modest, sober, bone dry hen
Lays eggs for nogs, then dies at 10.
All animals are strictly dry,
They sinless live and swiftly die,
But sinful, ginful, rum-soaked men
survive for three score years and ten.
And some of us, the mighty few,
Stay pickled till we're 92!"
Anonymous

How long can you live? Would you be surprised that you may can live to be 150? My research shows that this could be possible.

To be able to live a long life is a worthy goal, and we are fascinated by those who succeed. It appears that this has been the case since the dawning of history. In fact, Aristotle spoke of men living in Campania, a region in southern Italy, who lived to be in their eighties and married young virgins and had children by them. Also, the ancient Greek physician, Hippocrates, wrote of a man 100 years of age who married a girl of only thirty, and had many children by her. In addition, Phlegon, a Greek writer in the 2nd century, in his book *Long*

29

Lived Persons mentions the names of 117 centenarians who lived during the time of the Roman Empire. And according to Plutarch, Marcus Cato, a Roman statesman, lived to be at least ninety years of age. Further, Roman and Greek history records tell us that Terentia, who was the first wife of Cicero, lived to be 104, and Gorgias of Leontini, an ancient Greek philosopher and rhetorician, lived to be 107. And we must remember that all of these examples of longevity lived at a time when few people lived past the age of forty.

This fascination with longevity continues today. For instance, if you were to log on to the amazon.com website and search for books about "longevity", the results would show over 2,700 books, including *Secrets of Longevity, Longevity Made Simple, The Longevity Prescription,* and even *The Complete Idiot's Guide to Longevity.* These books may be designed to help you live a long life; but, unfortunately, the length of our lives is not necessarily in our control. The Roman philosopher Seneca points out that, "We are not summoned in the order of our birth registration." Life is a gift, but for some of us it is short. Mozart only lived to be thirty-five, and Egypt's King Tut died at nineteen, whereas others have lived to the ripe old age of 100 and beyond.

But under normal circumstances, how long should we live and better yet, how long can we live? The Book of Psalms in the Hebrew Bible says, "The days of our years are three score and ten." But on the other hand, the German philosopher Arthur Schopenhauer says, "In one of the *Vedic Upanishads (Oupnekhat, II.)* the natural length of human life is put down at one hundred years." Whereas, Albrecht von Haller, a Swiss physiologist, who lived in the 18th century, maintained that man might live to be 200. And a *Popular Science* article written in 1881 points out that one may live to be 150-160 years old and should be able to live to 200, but that man's lifestyle causes his premature death.

Also, there have been many theories and formulas created through the years to determine how long man can live. Some scientists have stated that the natural term of the life of an animal is five times the period needed for its development. Using this formula, it takes eighteen to twenty-one years for a human to reach full development; thus, his natural life span would be 90-105 years. Also, among the formulas that have been expounded upon, American biologist Raymond Pearl, who was a founder of biogerontology, stated that the maximum life span is inversely proportional to basal metabolic rate, whereby he concluded that the length of life was connected to the rate of life. In other words, the faster you live, the quicker your body wears out, which will shorten your life. Using Pearl's formula, some who live a fast pace may exhaust their heart and body as early as their forties; therefore, if one wants to live a long life, one must live at a slow pace.

Like Pearl, Christoph Wilhelm Hufeland, in his book *The Art of Prolonging Life,* speaks of a formula or theory which he calls "retardation of vital consumption". With this theory, it is contended that each one of us "is possessed with a certain quantity of vital power," and that life consists in the consumption of that power. He claims that this quantity of vital power can be exhausted, depending on the intensiveness of one's life. Hufeland goes on to say, "The less intensive the life of a being is, the longer will be its duration." In other words, the vital power in each of us is equivalent to a drum full of water. If we drain the drum quickly, then we will not live as long as if we drain the drum slowly.

Another theory which I found was attributed to the ancient Egyptians. They believed that the heart increased in size and weight from the time of birth until one was about fifty years old. And then, the heart began to decrease for the next fifty years in the same proportion. Thus, when one reached his 100th year, no more heart remained; consequently, human life ended.

Regardless of the formulas, theories, and varied beliefs of how long man can live, when compared to other inhabitants of this planet, man lives a decent life span. Consider the mayfly, who only lives a day. But there are many living things who live much longer than man. In 1497, a 350 pound fish was caught in a lake in Germany which bore a ring that was inscribed "I am the fish which was first of all put into the lake by the hands of the Governor of the Universe, Fredrick the Second, the 5th of October, 1230." This is pretty astounding, but if true, it would make the fish when caught 267 years old. The fish may have been old, but there are some living things that totally dwarf that fish and man's life span. For instance, there is a Bristlecone pine tree found in the White Mountains of California that is over 4,700 years old.

Most of us are familiar with Methuselah of the Hebrew Bible who is said to have lived 969 years. He lived to such an advanced age that his name has been used as a synonym for older creatures. In fact, scientists recently discovered what they believe is a gene that prolongs life, aptly it is named the Methuselah gene.

Methuselah has a rival though, with whom many people are not familiar — the Count of St. Germain. This gentleman's primary appearance was during the middle of the 18th century when he allegedly declared to the French Court of Louis XV that he was over 2,000 years old. The Count has been described as a scholar, musician, chemist, linguist, and adventurer. It has been contended that he possessed the secret to immortality on this earth. No one seemed to know where he came from, but he appeared to be rich and confident. The stories around the Count claim that he was actually the English scientist, Francis Bacon, and that he, as Francis Bacon, was really the true author of the Plays of Shakespeare, and not Shakespeare himself. Claims have continued that Francis Bacon did not really die in 1626, but, instead, he became the Count incarnate. Furthermore, it seems that the Count never *really* dies but continues to emerge into different people as the ages pass. It has been said that over the thousands of years that he claimed to have lived, that he was actually Plato, Merlin the Magician of King Arthur's Court, and a priest of the lost civilization of Atlantis, in addition to being Francis Bacon. After his appearance in the 18th century, the Count disappeared as suddenly as he had appeared. But there are those who believe that he still lives today. I've read that Annie Besant, an English women's rights' activist and writer, said that she met the Count in 1896, and that one C. W. Leadbetter met the Count in 1926. The Count was also the subject of a television series in the 1970-80's and is featured in video games today.

The stories of the Count are quite bizarre, and any reasonable person would dispel how long the Count may have actually lived, but throughout history, there have been many stories as to how long certain people have lived. However, most modern writings claim that the oldest person ever recorded was Jeanne Louise Calment of France, who lived to be 122. Ms. Calment, who died in 1997, lived an extraordinary long life and was active throughout her life — at 85, she took up fencing, rode a bike at 100, and even recorded a CD at 121. If Jeanne Calment lived to be 122 years old, particularly as active as she was, I wondered why couldn't there be others who lived longer, but maybe not as long as Methuselah or the Count of St. Germain? So I set out to pursue the answer to this question, and I was surprised at what I found.

It appears that there may have been many others who actually did live longer than Jeanne Calment. For instance, Thomas Parr, an Englishman known as "Old Tom Parr", allegedly reached the age of 152. Records show that Parr was born in 1483 and died in 1635. He did not marry until he was eighty years old, and amazingly, had an affair at age 100, begetting an illegitimate child. Upon the death of his first wife, he married again at age 122. When King Charles I of England learned of this aged man, he brought him to London where he was treated royally. But, it has been said that this extra-ordinary treatment bore such a change on Parr's life that it may have brought about his untimely death, for he died shortly after his visit to London. "Old Tom Parr" was so lauded for his longevity by the King that he was buried in Westminister Abbey, the burial place of Kings and Lords.

In addition to "Old Tom Parr", I found many others who lived beyond the age of Ms. Calment. For instance, among the ancient writings which have been saved through the centuries, there is a letter by the Syrian rhetorician, Lucian of Samosata, who lived during the reign of Roman Emperor Marcus Aurelius in the 2nd century A.D. written to his friend, Quintillus, on his birthday. In his writing, Lucian stated that it had been said that Nestor, who was considered the wisest of the Greeks, lived three times the natural age of man. He went on to say that many others lived extraordinary long lives, including Arganthonius, King of the Tartessians, who lived to be 150 years old. And Lucian further relates that "among the historians, Etesibius dropped dead as he was walking, at the age of 124."

Extreme interest with longevity was particularly prevalent during the 19th century. During this period, there was a book written by Dr. George M. Gould and Dr. Walter

L. Pyle entitled *Anomalies and Curiosities of Medicine,* which was primarily about siamese twins, midgets, and other anomalies, but there is a chapter devoted to longevity. Drs. Gould and Pyle were apparently distinguished medical doctors and had performed much research for their book so the information should be somewhat reliable. Included in their chapter on longevity, they point out that the English Registrar-General's Department gave tables of life expectancy in England for the periods 1871-80 showing that eighty-two males and 225 females out of 1,000,000 were alive at the age of 100. They also note that on the register of Cheshire County, England there is shown that one Thomas Hough died at the age of 141 in 1591. In addition, they list Thomas Wishart of Scotland, stating that he died in 1760 at age 124, who had, amazingly, chewed tobacco for 117 years.

Gould and Pyle noted that France had the honor of claiming the oldest woman of their times, with the lady having attained 150 years of age. Furthermore, they pointed out that in Italy in 76 A. D., one hundred and twenty-four persons had attained the age of 100 and upward; two were 125, four were 130, four more were from 135 to 137, and three were 140. In addition, they also wrote of two people in Hungary who had lived in earlier times; one reached the age of 187 and the other 172. They also spoke of Louisa Truxo of South America who died in 1780 at the age of 175, and of a Russian woman who was living in Moscow in 1848 who was 168 years of age. In America, Gould and Pyle claimed that Dr. William Hotchkiss of St. Louis, Missouri reached the age of 140, and that Noah Raby of New Jersey was alive at the age of 123.

Another source I've found regarding longevity written during the 19th century was *Barkham Burrough's*

Encyclopedia of Astounding Facts and Useful Information published in 1889. This book states that in Russia in 1825 eight hundred and forty-eight men had reached upward of 100 years of age; thirty-two had passed their 120th year; and four were still alive who ranged from 130 to 135 in age.

But, the most comprehensive book that I discovered was *Records of Longevity* by Thomas Bailey written in 1856. Bailey compiled a list of over two thousand people whose ages ranged from 80 to 185, with many having a short description of their lives. Included in his book are Francis Ange, who was born in England and died in Maryland in 1767 at the age of 134. Also, Bailey describes a woman named "Mother Goose" who was living in Oxford, England in 1673 at 120 years of age. In his long compilation, Bailey also listed a Mr. Gillett of Augusta, Maine who died in 1814 at the age of 124. He further cited Jonathan Hartop of the village of Yorkshire, England who died in 1791 at the age of 138 and also stated that St. Mungo, according to the Archbishop of St. Andrew's, lived to be 185. And among his examples of long lives, Bailey tells of a tombstone in a churchyard in England bearing the following inscription: "Here Lieth the body of William Edwards, of the Cacreg, who departed this life on the 24th of February, *Anno Domini,* 1668, *anno setatis suse* one hundred and sixty eight."

Of his massive list, the most convincing person that Bailey described was Henry Jenkins of Yorkshire, England, who, Bailey says died at the age of 169 in 1670. Bailey not only writes of Jenkins, but includes a picture of Jenkins in his book which shows an elderly, stately, and healthy-looking gentleman. Bailey cites that Jenkins' extra-ordinary age was supported by testimonies from elders who knew Jenkins during his life-time. These elders stated that

Jenkins was a butler, and that in the latter years of his life, became a fisherman and would often swim in the river, even after he was a hundred years of age. As further proof of Jenkins' longevity, Bailey states that Jenkins once gave a deposition in 1665 in which he stated he was 157 years of age. Several years after Jenkins' death, a monument was erected to perpetuate his memory which also supports his age at the time of his death.

Other sources that I found substantiate that Jeanne Calment was not the oldest living person. For instance, *New Goals for Old Age* published in 1943, mentions that C. J. Drakenberg, a Danish man, was 145 when he died in 1772. And Louis Philippe McCarty tells us in his book *Health, Happiness and Longevity* published in 1890 that the oldest human being living in the United States at the time of his book was an old Indian named Gabriel who lived one hundred miles south of San Francisco, California who was at least 146 years old.

In fact, as recent as 2010 it was reported that there was a woman Antisa Khvichava who lived in a remote mountain village in the former Soviet Republic of Georgia who was born on July 8, 1880 which would make her 130 years old at that time. And the future may bring us many who live beyond the age of Ms. Calment if the prediction of Dr. Aubrey De Grey is correct. De Grey has pronounced that the first person to live for 1,000 years will be born in the next two decades. So who knows how long someone can live or will live? But the sources I have mentioned have convinced me that there may have been many more individuals who have lived longer than Jeanne Calment who supposedly, was the oldest living person ever recorded.

One thing that is important when discussing the

subject of longevity is that longevity is not to be confused with life expectancy. Longevity deals with one's life span, whereas life expectancy is the average age at death of all individuals in a country, state, county, or group, taking into account diseases, congenital defects, accidents, and the like.

Using life expectancy as our guide, if you live beyond the life expectancy of your generation, you will have had a long life. In prehistoric times, life expectancy may have been as low as fourteen years. During those times, life was a constant struggle to find food and shelter, and man was much more exposed to the elements and dangers. Therefore, many lost out very early in life; thus, if you made it to forty, you could be considered old since very few reached that age. As man became more civilized and began to leave the hunting way of life for agriculture, he was able to increase his life expectancy. But even as civilizations sprung up and life expectancy increased, the problems of living a long life still existed.

Accordingly, in the days of ancient Greece, life expectancy had increased from a low of fourteen years when man was nomadic to 29.4 years. And by the time Rome reached its peak, life expectancy had increased to about forty years; however, many did live past forty. For instance, the ancient Greek philosopher, Plato, lived to be eighty, and Marcus Cato, a Roman statesman, lived to be at least ninety years old. In fact, Augustus Caesar's wife, Livia, lived to be eighty-six. However, we must remember that life expectancy doesn't just continue to go up; it can go down. For example, after Rome fell and the Dark Ages set in, life expectancy dropped back down to an all-time low and did not begin to recover for hundreds of years.

Even as late as the 18th century, Voltaire said that

the estimated life expectancy of human life during his time was only twenty-two years. This was probably because infant mortality in the cities at that time was as high as fifty percent. In fact, until 1850, only one-half of the children born in the United States would reach the age of five. Even in 1901, life expectancy at birth in the United States was still only about fifty years of age. However, today, life expectancy has been greatly increased by the reduction of mortality in babies and children, by the prevention and cure of diseases, advancement in surgery, and by better nutrition and hygiene. Fortunately, by 2010, life expectancy had risen to 78.3 in the United States. Thus, today, if you live beyond seventy-nine, you will have made it to a ripe old age. In fact, I find it amazing how proud an eighty year old is of their age. In the last year, I have had at least three octogenarians make sure in our conversations that I knew they were eighty years old or older. They appear to be very pleased with themselves that they have joined those who have reached the extra-ordinary long life span.

Even though we have been successful in increasing life expectancy, there were times in history when some cultures didn't worry about longevity or life expectancy; they took care of the problem themselves. For instance, on the isle of Ceos, no one was to live beyond sixty, for as reported by Plutarch, "there was once a law that appears to have commanded those who were sixty years of age to drink hemlock..." Of course, that was the poison that killed Socrates. Also, Herodotus, in his travels, spoke of the Padaian Indians who he claimed were pastoral and ate raw flesh. They practiced the following custom: "Whenever any of their tribe falls ill, whether it be woman or man... his nearest associates put him to death." They contended that if he continued to remain ill, it would spoil his flesh. Herodotus goes on to state that in addition to the ill, they treated elders in the same fashion, "if a man has come to old age they slay him and feast upon him; but very few of them come to be reckoned as old, for they kill every one who falls into sickness, before he reaches old age."

Fortunately, we do not have to worry today about being put to death like the Padaians because of sickness or old age; but, most of us will probably not live extraordinary long lives, but instead, will live within the confines of life expectancy. However, history is replete with facts and figures that point to the possibility that any one of us may live an extraordinary long life. But what are the theories or recipes that have been given to attain this extraordinary longevity?

One of the main theories is heredity. For example, the descendants of "Old Tom Parr" (who lived to be 152) appeared to enjoy long lives themselves. We don't know about his ancestors, but his grandson, John Newell of Michael's Town, Ireland, is said to have lived to the ripe old age of 127. Also, his great-grandson, Robert Parr, died at the age of 124, and other members of the Parr family lived beyond 100 years of age.

Aside from heredity, another theory is that marriage may have something to do with longevity. The philosopher Immanuel Kant said that he "found in the whole list of persons who had lived to an extraordinary age (120-160) not a single one unmarried." However, this may be refuted for Hryhoriy Nester of the Ukraine who died in 2007 at age 116, credited his longevity to having never been married.

Also a theory for longevity could be as a result of a person's career, such as the performing arts. Gould and Pyle in their *Anomalies and Curiosities of Medicine* stated that there are several instances of longevity in Roman actresses which have been recorded. For example, the

Roman actress, Luceja, performed for one hundred years and made an appearance at the age of 112, and the dancer, Copiola, was to have danced before Augustus Caesar when she was over ninety. Even in the modern world, many actors and actresses have lived long lives, such as Katharine Hepburn, who lived to be ninety-six, and Bob Hope and George Burns, who both lived to be 100.

Also, artists are among the ranks of having long lives. For instance, Grandma Moses was still painting at 100, and Picasso painted up until his death at ninety-one. And Picasso may have explained a reason for artists having long lives. Picasso, a prolific painter, who often worked in total silence for twelve hours at a time from afternoon until the early morning hours, when asked if he got tired of standing so long in one spot as he painted, he answered, "No. That is why painters live so long. While I work I leave my body outside the door, the way Moslems take off their shoes before entering the mosque."

Maybe virtue has something to do with longevity. Chan Seug, who wrote a chapter that appeared in Sir John Sinclair's book *Code of Health and Longevity,* said these words: "They then who would prolong their life must immediately study to be virtuous. A regular care of the body, supported by the constant practice of virtue, will make that constitution hail and strong, from whence will follow a long and happy life."

Another theory to attain an extraordinary long life may be from what we eat or drink. For instance, honey has been referred to as the "juice of life". The Greek philosopher Democritus, when asked at 100 years of age, how he had lived so long, he stated, "by the application of oil without, and honey within." Even in the modern world, Dr. Eva Crane, who was a noted writer and expert on bees and beekeeping, contended that "Old Tom Parr's" longevity may have been due to eating honey since he was a beekeeper, as well as a farmer. Also among food and drink, sour milk has been linked to longevity. Yogurt would fall into this category. It has been said that in 1896, there were at least 5,000 people who were 100 or more in age who lived primarily on soured milk in Serbia, Bulgaria, and Romania. The sour milk theory is also set forth in the book, *The Bacillus of Long Life* by Landon Douglas which was published in 1911 in which Douglas describes that there were many people in countries in which soured milk was their main diet, and as a result, the "age limit for human beings seems to be very much extended." He draws the conclusion that "there is a direct connection between the use of soured milk and longevity."

Even setting goals may help us live a long life. John D. Rockefeller, Sr. set two goals early in life — one to be rich and the other to live to be 100. He made his first goal by becoming one of the wealthiest men in the world. He almost made his other goal, but not quite, in that he died at age ninety-seven.

One's religion may even play a role; for instance, I read that Quakers live longer than others, and more recently, I read that Mormons also live longer lives than most.

Also, among the many obituaries, newspaper articles, books, and other material that I accumulated over the years, I found numerous recipes by individuals which they claimed as their secret for their long lives — some quite bizarre. For instance, Bernard le Bovier de Fontenelle, who died in his hundredth year, attributed his longevity to eating strawberries; Edward Rondthaler, who died at 104, gave a daily cold shower for over ninety years as his recipe for a long life; Thomas Hobbes, who in 1670 at age eighty-two published *Behemoth,* and at age eighty-seven wrote his autobiography in verse, dying at ninety-two, sang at night behind closed doors for his health and longevity. And aside from his goals, Rockefeller also had a recipe that he attributed for his long life – a round of golf and a tablespoon of olive oil each day.

Another recipe was given by Susie Gibson of Tuscumbia, Alabama, who celebrated her 113th birthday in 2002. She advocated her longevity, in part, to a daily dose of vinegar mixed with pickle juice, whereas Eva Rayo Potosme of Nicaragua, who claimed in 2003 that she was 116, gave her love for beef soup with vegetables as her basis for longevity. And Pearl Gordon of Madison, Mississippi, who celebrated her 103rd birthday in 2001, credited her longevity to eating nutty bars and drinking Dr. Pepper.

The baby doctor, Benjamin Spock, whose best selling book, *Baby & Child,* influenced the raising of children for generations, lived to be ninety-four. His long life could be attributed to his routine of rowing, meditation, yoga, massages, and dining on brown rice, soup and vegetables.

And among others who gave their recipes were Eva Morris of Stone, England, who died just six days short of her 115th birthday in 2000. She attributed her longevity to whiskey and boiled onions. Kamato Hongo of Japan, who turned 116 in 2003, had an unusual routine of sleeping for two days and staying awake for the next two days; she also snacked on unrefined brown sugar and attributed her long life to "not moping around."

Meritt M. Burnett, of Washington, D.C., who died at

109 in 1999, attributed his longevity to doing all things in moderation. But, amazingly, he smoked cigars until he was 107. And Stanley Kunitz, whom I mentioned earlier, said the secret to his longevity was his attitude. He said, "I'm curious, I'm active. I garden and I write and I drink martinis." He died in 2006 at the age of 100.

Walter Breuning of Montana revealed his rules for a long life shortly before his death in 2011 at the age of 114 when he said, "embrace change; eat two meals a day; work as long as you can; help others, and don't fear death."

Even though the baseball player, Satchel Paige, who pitched his final inning at age fifty-nine, did not live an extraordinarily long life, dying at age seventy-five, wrote a guide to longevity for us: "(1) Avoid fried meats, which angry up the blood; (2) If your stomach disputes you, lie down and pacify it with cool thoughts; (3) Keep the juices flowing by jangling around gently as you move; (4) Go very light on the vices, such as carrying on in society. The social rumble ain't restful; (5) Avoid running at all times; and (6) Don't look back. Something might be gaining on you."

Probably all of the people named above are now gone, but I'm sure there are many people today who have recipes which they are using in an attempt to live to a ripe old age, long beyond life-expectancy. One of those is the actress, Suzanne Somers. She said that she was shooting to reach 110 years of age with a recipe consisting of daily vaginal estriol hormone injections, rubbing estrogen on one arm and progesterone on the other arm, taking forty pills each morning (fifteen with a smoothie), and then twenty more pills at bedtime.

Even though there are many theories and recipes of yesterday and today on how to live a long life, Thomas Bailey and Hufeland give us insight on possibly the best way to live a long life. Bailey said that temperance, industry, and exercise are the three great elements of longevity. He pointed out that, "A few slothful men have attained to extreme old age, and so have a few gluttons and drunkards...but for the most part...an incomparably greater proportion, long livers have been distinguished for their sober and industrious habits." And Hufeland, in the 18th century, gave us possibly one of the best recipes to attain an extraordinarily long life. He describes a person destined for an extraordinary long life, among other things, as being "... serene, loquacious, active, susceptible of joy, love, and hope; but insensible to... hatred, anger, and avarice." Their passions never become "violent or destructive". They are "fond also of employment, optimistic, a friend to nature." They have no "thirst after honors or riches", and they do not worry about tomorrow. Their "pulse is slow and regular." They have a good appetite and enjoy dining, but they do not "eat merely for the sake of eating".

One last thought on longevity. Will Durant tells us that the primitive natives of New Britain believed that a mistake was made by their gods in that snakes were supposed to die as man does now, and that a man was to be able to molt like snakes and that he would not die. But the messenger sent by the gods got everything mixed up, and the opposite occurred. Except for this mistake, maybe we wouldn't have to worry about longevity; we could merely shed our skin every now and then and live forever.

CHAPTER 4

MEDICINE — ITS HISTORY,
ITS MIRACLES,
ITS CURSES

Medicine: "Any substance or preparation
used in treating disease.
The science and art
dealing with the prevention, cure,
or alleviation of disease."

Webster's Dictionary

It's no doubt that today modern medicine plays a major role in helping us live longer and is certainly giving us more quality in our lives. However, I felt I could not fully understand medicine today, and how thankful we should be for modern medicine, unless I delved into its history.

In the past, attempting to live a long life was hard to do. Even under the best of circumstances, diseases were always ready to pounce upon you, to invade your body, crippling or killing you. But, as we look back in history, there were those who knew man had the ability to conquer most of these diseases, but it would be a long, rough, rocky road to do so and for medicine to get where it is today.

Medicine for man in his primitive state relied mainly on religion to attempt to conquer diseases and other afflictions. Medical problems were believed to be caused by hostile spirits or the anger of the gods, and that only magic or prayers could remove the disease. Fortunately, man moved past this stage in history, and medicine progressed with it; however, religion and ignorance would continue to hold it back for centuries.

As civilizations formed and man left the hunting and nomadic life, medicine would improve, even though at times the practices were bizarre by today's standards. For instance, physicians in Babylon treated internal ailments by fumigation by forcing smoke from a fire into the anus, mouth, and nose. Also, diagnosis and treatment may have been determined by hepatoscopy, which is the religious practice by priests whereby they inspected the entrails and livers of sacrificed animals and compared them to the illness of the human patient. Physicians even relied on astrology for treatment of diseases and various ailments.

Moreover, in ancient Egypt physicians used vomiting, enemas, diuretics, and bleeding as a means of treatment. Some of the medicines which were concocted by the Egyptians were derived from worms, insects, snakes, elephants, lions, camels, crocodiles, hyaenas, and even from man himself.

These types of medicines and treatments continued through the Middle Ages and some even as recently as two hundred years ago, and many times, the medical treatments were worse than the maladies themselves. In one year, Louis XIII of France in the 17th century was bled forty-seven times, received 215 enemas, and swallowed 212 drugs.

Even if some of the treatments and medical practices were successful, people in the past still had to contend with plagues, diseases, and fevers which limited the ability for them to live a long life. In 429 B.C., Pericles, the renowned Athenian statesman of ancient Greece, would die of a plague along with a major portion of the Greek population. Another plague, the Black Death, which began in China, made its way to Europe in 1340, and by 1349, had killed up to two-thirds of the population of Europe and England. In 1665 the Black Death returned, killing over 68,000 people in London alone; Samuel Pepys, in the month of August of that year, would write in his diary, "... the town growing so unhealthy that a man cannot depend on living two days... Dr. Burnett, my physician, is this morning dead of the plague...But, Lord! How everybody looks, and discourse in the street is of death and nothing else, and few people going up and down, that the town is like a place distressed and forsaken."

Unfortunately, the populace of England was so simple-minded and the medical community was so ignorant, they would blame the Black Death on such causes as eating radishes, caviar, anchovies, pigeons, and possibly drinking strong beer. Also, as a preventative, some believed that posies of herbs, if carried on their person, would protect them from the plague, giving rise to the childhood game of "Ring Around the Roses". It was even rumored that syphilis would ward off the plague, causing the men of London to storm the brothels.

Besides these plagues, other diseases were rampant throughout history. Smallpox, one of the most dreaded diseases of all, ravaged ancient Egypt. In fact, pustules have been found on the mummy of Ramses V who ruled Egypt from 1149 to 1145 B.C. And also Roman legions contracted smallpox in 165 A.D. and spread the disease throughout the empire killing as many as two thousand people per day. Until modern times, each generation that has come down through the ages has been faced with smallpox. Voltaire calculated during his lifetime that in a hundred persons who came into the world, at least sixty contracted smallpox, and of that sixty, twenty would die, and twenty would be left with disagreeable marks. In the 18th century alone, sixty million Europeans would die from smallpox. There was no exemption for the royalty either; from 1712 to 1715, three heirs to the French throne would die of smallpox. Even in America in 1776, one-half of the Continental Army under George Washington would be affected by an epidemic of smallpox.

Another dreaded disease in the past was tuberculosis. This disease would continue to ravage mankind for hundreds of years and is still a menace today in some parts of the world. In 1638, it would kill John Harvard [for whom Harvard University was named] at the age of thirty-one. In the 19th century, Ralph Waldo Emerson would lose his wife, two brothers, and his friend, Henry David Thoreau, to tuberculosis. D. H. Lawrence was dying of tuberculosis in the 1920's as he was writing *Lady Chatterley's Lover*, and George Orwell was dying from it while writing *Nineteen Eighty-four* in the 1940's.

And if you didn't get smallpox or tuberculosis, there was yellow fever to contend with. This dreaded disease causes the body to become so jaundiced prior to death that it has been given the name "yellow fever". There were many epidemics of yellow fever in the 18th and 19th centuries in various cities throughout the United States, including New York City, Charleston, New Orleans, and Memphis, Tennessee. In 1793, the future First Lady Dolly Madison would lose her husband, John Todd, a Quaker lawyer, in the yellow fever epidemic in Philadelphia, leaving her a widow with two young children. During the Philadelphia epidemic, the populace and the medical community, like in London during the Black Death, were so ignorant in combating the fever, they would try soaking masks in garlic juice, vinegar, and camphor in an attempt to avoid the disease, all to no avail.

There were many other diseases that mankind faced in the past. Among these was measles which was brought to the New World by European explorers and colonists, and in addition to affecting its carriers, it would devastate vast Indian populations throughout the Americas. Another disease was pneumonia which has killed countless numbers of human beings throughout the ages, including William Henry Harrison, who died of the disease only one month after taking the office of the presidency of the United States. Also, scarlet fever, according to the famous muckraker, Ida Tarbell, was more dreaded by mothers in the 1800's than was smallpox in that smallpox may scar, but scarlet fever would usually kill. There was also the mosquito-borne malaria which originated in the swamps and killed thousands during the summer months. In addition, history tells us that typhus killed President Zachary Taylor only sixteen months into his presidency. And most of us are aware of polio, which killed or crippled thousands in the United States in the first half of the 20th century, including President Franklin Delano Roosevelt, who in 1921 was crippled for life as a result of this disease.

Today, the plagues, along with many of the dreaded diseases of the past, have abated or disappeared all together because of the knowledge and practices brought about by modern medicine. But even though medicine continued to improve over time, there were still many roadblocks and backward practices that were used. One of the roadblocks was the inability for physicians to examine cadavers to learn about the human body. The Roman Catholic Church and various medieval governments opposed the dissecting of cadavers; thus, the medical community was forced to use unconventional means for their study — by "body snatching". When a cadaver was obtained through this means, a dissection would take place, and drawings were made for the physicians to use. In 1510, Leonardo da Vinci, famously known for his "Mona Lisa", became one of the primary forces in the advancement of medicine by producing a book of drawings of dissected cadavers. Now physicians could finally have some sort of access to real human anatomy, rather than relying on animals and guessing what might be in humans.

Among the backward practices were astrology and bloodletting. Astrology would slowly leave the medical field, but it has remained with the public throughout the years, and even today, we see it in horoscopes and other practices. However, even though it is rarely seen today, bloodletting was a major treatment for thousands of years.

This archaic practice was to remove blood from a patient to cure or prevent ailments or disease. It was performed through two main means: the draining of blood by cutting into a vein or by the use of leeches. Drawing blood from the veins was performed with a tourniquet applied above the elbow and the patient gripping a stick so that the vein would swell, and then a sharp pointed instrument thrust into the vein in order to drain the blood from the body. In its earliest years of practice, it was performed mainly by barbers. In fact, the barber poles of today represent this former practice in their profession. The pole represents the stick which was gripped by the patient to promote bleeding from the arm, while the white stripes on the pole represent the tourniquet used to increase the pressure on the vein of the limb to be opened. The red and blue stripes represent the blood - blue when in the vein, and red when drawn. Bloodletting by barbers continued up until the 18th century when physician surgeons finally took complete charge of the procedure.

Bloodletting by the use of leeches was performed by a physician placing a leech (a shiny worm-like freshwater parasite) on the patient, with the leech attaching itself to the skin and sucking the blood from the patient. Most leeches used in America were imported from Europe. Small children would have been given one or two leeches, whereas twenty to fifty leeches would be used on adults. A leech would usually take an hour to reach its fill and would drop off on its own.

Bloodletting was used for almost every ailment, including asthma, indigestion, epilepsy, gout, and other common ailments and diseases. Unfortunately, bloodletting was many times an example of the cure being worse than the cause. In fact, we may have even lost our greatest statesman to this practice. In his last illness, George Washington was bled four times in two days for what may have been only a common ailment from exposure to the wind and rain. Unfortunately, this excessive bleeding probably contributed to his death, whereas, today, a mere visit to a general practitioner would have cured George Washington's ailment with a simple injection of antibiotics or other medicine, allowing him to live a much longer life. However, George Washington was not the only victim of this practice. In 1754, it was calculated by a European physician that 40,000 deaths in France were as a result of excessive bloodletting. Even so, the practice of bloodletting continued in a major way throughout the western world until about 1830 when it began a slow decline until it basically disappeared at the beginning of the 20th century. However, bleeding is still used today, but only in special circumstances.

Even though medicine would languish throughout history, the era of modern medicine did not really begin until Edward Jenner's discovery that led to the smallpox vaccine at the end of the 18ᵗʰ century. Jenner had noticed that milkmaids who had been infected with cowpox from the udder of a cow were not susceptible to smallpox; but even with this discovery, it would still be over eighty years before the next major step in the progress of medicine occurred when it was discovered by Louis Pasteur that inoculation of an animal with a weak amount of the disease may cause a slight attack of the disease, but after recovery, the animal thereafter had an immunity against the disease. Through his experiments, Pasteur concluded that most diseases were caused by micro-organisms.

Later, Pasteur's conclusion was applied by Joseph Lister, an English surgeon using antiseptics to kill germs in surgery procedures. Lister reached his own conclusion that air is not bad in itself, but that minute particles which are suspended in air can be germs which cause infections in wounds and surgery. The name Lister is still with us today, for the antiseptic "Listerine" is named for this gentleman.

With the discoveries of Jenner, Pasteur, Lister, and others, modern medicine, as we know it today, would finally begin. It was now known that germs carried disease, and that the germs could be carried through the air. Also by now, the medical community knew that germs thrived in filth and unsanitary conditions, and that the transmission of disease may be carried by the flea, the louse, the bedbug, the house fly, the mosquito, and the tick. But it would be the building of the Panama Canal in the early 1900's which would lead to the proof of the transmission of diseases by insects, thereby resulting in the solution of ridding man from the horrors and death brought on by malaria, yellow fever, and other like diseases.

Prior to the canal being built, to reach California by sea from the eastern part of the United States required sailing to the southern-most tip of South America around Cape Horn. Not only was this an extremely long journey by ship, it was also very dangerous. However, it was known that a canal could probably be constructed across the Isthmus of Panama, which would substantially shorten the distance to California. But no one had taken this endeavor to task. It would be the discovery of gold at Sutter's Mill, California in 1848 that would give the spark necessary to create a true demand for a canal.

A French company would try to build the canal, but they would fail. In addition to financial problems, they lost twenty thousand employees, dying of yellow fever, malaria, dysentery, typhus, and other tropical diseases. After eight years of these problems, the French company went bankrupt and abandoned the project. It was then that the United States decided to take up the challenge. In 1907 President Theodore Roosevelt put the entire project under the U.S. Army Engineers which resulted in the completion of the Panama Canal in 1914. However, once again, as with the French, diseases struck the workers; but now, with the knowledge that mosquitoes carried these diseases, that unsanitary conditions bred germs which caused these diseases, and as a result of the medical knowledge from Jenner, Pasteur, Lister, and others, the U.S. engineers attacked the problems by eliminating the mosquitoes and their habitat, which virtually eliminated the diseases. This gave absolute proof that unsanitary conditions and disease-carrying insects were the culprits behind many of the plagues that had wrought mankind through the ages.

Around the same time as the Panama Canal was being built, modern medicine began to take giant strides in many areas. It was as if someone turned on a lightbulb at the onset of the 20th century. One medical success after another would begin to occur. Among others, aspirin was developed; mosquito controls were put into place; compulsory vaccination laws were passed; better dairy practices were legislated; the canning of meats and vegetables was introduced; penicillin was discovered, as well as other antibiotics; the pap smear was developed; x-rays became a normal means of diagnosis; new surgical techniques appeared; the electrocardiograph machine was invented; hypertension and heart disease were linked; insulin for diabetes was discovered; pacemakers were invented; kidney dialysis was introduced; artificial hip and knee replacements and organ transplants began; discoveries were made regarding human DNA; and pills were developed to avert the causes of heart disease.

Thus, the progress of medicine over this time became almost a continuous success with leaps and bounds of inventions, treatments, and cures right up until today. Hardly a day goes by that I do not hear of some new medical discovery or treatment. Over the last one hundred years, medicine has improved life more than in the entire 6,000 years before. In 1904 life expectancy in the United States was only forty-seven years; whereas, today, life expectancy has increased almost thirty years and has now reached seventy-nine years. In addition, infant mortality has dropped from 122 per thousand in 1900 to only 6.3 per thousand today.

Moreover, modern medicine still continues to produce miracles and has solved many of mankind's maladies that he had suffered throughout history. It has increased our ability to live longer, is allowing us to live healthier lives for a longer period than ever, and it has given life more quality.

I realize that the medical community has not cured all problems and diseases, nor developed a cure for the common cold and other like ailments. But for the miracles they have given us, we must be thankful. The successes have been outstanding, but, unfortunately, they still have not developed pills or elixirs that can give us an outlook on life that will keep us from growing old like my father.

That being said, modern medicine may be doing such a good job, it is now resulting in curses for many. Imagine you are 90 years old; you are on ten different medicines which the doctors have prescribed to keep your body functioning; you are now in a nursing home; you can hardly recognize your family members as they come to visit you; you wear diapers as you did when you were two years old; you are feeble; and you have no quality in your life any longer. You share a room with someone that you do not know or even like; someone down the hall may be screaming; your clothes are tampered with by others in the nursing home; and you don't even know where you are yourself. Only death will alleviate this situation; but there may be hope that you will never reach this stage if you will only strive to do what it takes to stay young and not grow old.

CHAPTER 5

THE HEALTHY LIFE?

"The way to keep healthy
is to
know one's own constitution..."
Cicero

The medical world seems to be doing its part to help us live a long life and help us maintain our health. But how are we as individuals doing in this regard? Are we living a healthy life? And what about those who I was studying, did they live a healthy life? Does our living a healthy life affect our ability to live longer lives and will it keep us young? Asking these questions, I turned my project to the study of health. I first defined what I believed was considered a healthy life. It appeared simple and obvious — one who gets plenty of sleep, doesn't smoke, eats in moderation a balanced diet, regularly exercises, maintains good hygiene, and is responsible in his consumption of alcohol.

Like my study of medicine, in order to completely understand the value of living a healthy life, and its probable necessity in order to obtain a long life, to do this, I felt compelled to study how man has dealt with his own health practices throughout the ages. Knowing that we are faced with a real problem with obesity today, I began with diet and what role it plays in order for us to live long lives, give us energy and vitality like Hulda Crooks, and possibly keep us from growing old like my father.

It appears that the relationship between diet and health has been recognized throughout the ages. In the

19th century, the French physiologist, Jean Pierre Flourens, said, "man kills himself rather than dies", and this, coupled with the old English proverb that says *a man may dig his grave with his teeth,* appears to be appropriate in today's world. Amazingly, about sixty-eight percent of American adults are overweight. Of those who are overweight, almost thirty-four percent are considered obese. Just look around. I am astounded by the number of people I see daily who are obese. If you need further proof, just visit your local Wal-Mart. Moreover, I recently read about a forty-nine year old woman who weighs 700 pounds and considered to be the fattest woman in the world. She became so fat that she has been bed-ridden for three years. Her condition is directly related to her diet. She said she grew up on soul food and never watched what she ate. Of course, soul food consists of lots of fried meats, gravy, breads, and vegetables cooked with fat. With three meals a day of this kind of food, along with a few snacks, obesity is guaranteed in just about everyone. I also read of a man who weighed 784 pounds, whose consumption of food was 20,000 calories each day. He was unable to walk and had to use a motorized chair. He was so fat that a forklift was necessary to lift him and transfer him to an ambulance when he was forced to be hospitalized for an ailment.

So how did all of this obesity come about? One of the causes today appears to mirror the "fast food" business. In the past, food was treasured but not worshiped. However, in 1961 with the take-over of McDonald's by Ray Kroc, "fast food" became a way of life. Kroc got richer, and Americans got fatter. In 1964, Burger King moved into the "fast-food" business, and others have followed such as KFC. "Upsizing" became an everyday word. Food has become so popular that there is a restaurant on practically every corner, and servings at almost all restaurants have gotten larger through the years. Food even made Julia Child a television star. You can't go to the hardware store or the drug store to get your medicine to keep you in decent health without having food being presented to you. For instance, these stores will have candy and other snacks at the check-out counters luring you like the Sirens of Greek mythology. Of course, grocery stores are still growing bigger every day. It is obvious that this obsession with food by those who sell and by those who eat has led us to the obesity problems of today.

What is surprising is that the ancients seemed to have handled obesity better than we moderns do. For example, in Sparta maintaining health was a way of life. If a man's belly swelled indecently he might be publicly rebuked by the government. Also, the Egyptians believed that the majority of diseases came from the digestion of food and extensive eating, and they used purging as a means to offset overeating. Even the ancient physician, Hippocrates, who is often called the father of western medicine, focused on not eating too much as a way to maintain health, and in particular, elders' eating habits. He declared that, "Older persons need less fuel (food) than the young." Modern guidelines would also agree with this philosophy.

In the 16th century there appeared a series of essays regarding diet by an Italian gentleman, Luigi Cornaro. At age eighty-three, he wrote his first essay discussing his ailments that he had suffered when he was a young man. He said that in his younger years he was wealthy enough to live the life of luxury regarding food and drink, and this he did, but at age forty he realized that it was destroying his health. Suffering from pains in his stomach and side, gout, low fever, and thirst, he was advised by his physicians that he should live a temperate and orderly life if he wished to forego his problems and recover his health. As a result, he developed a diet whereby he "was not to partake of any foods, solid or liquid", except those that might be prescribed for invalids, and then only in "small quantities." Cornaro's regimen resulted in his total intake of food of only twelve ounces each day with fourteen ounces of wine. Within a year, he declared himself cured, and his health continued to remain superb from that point forward. After forty-three years on his diet, he said his mind was clear; he no longer suffered melancholy and other like maladies as when he was younger; his senses were sharper; he was in such good physical shape that he could mount a horse with no help; he could run upstairs; and he was cheerful at all times.

Three years later at age eighty-six Cornaro wrote a second essay and reiterated the success of his dieting, stating that he was still in good health, strong, and joyous. Five years later at age ninety-one, once again, Cornaro wrote another essay. He reaffirmed that his health was still excellent and that he walked and sang each day. At age ninety-two, Cornaro reported again that he was still in good health and looked forward to living to the age of 100. Little is known about Cornaro after this last report, but it is believed that he made it to 100, fulfilling his wish. However, one must wonder that if Cornaro lived today, could he have succeeded as he did then, with the abounding "Big Macs", "Whoppers", and "biggie-size fries" and other temptations of food from every direction? But, his life and his essays appear to show that diet habits certainly can help maintain one's health and give vitality and even a positive outlook on life, for he assured us in his eighties and nineties that he was strong, had lots of energy, was joyful and cheerful.

Cornaro's essays made such an impact for the future regarding diet and health that a hundred years later, Leonardus Lessius, a Jesuit of Louvaine University, was so impressed by Cornaro's essays, that he wrote a book which was published in 1613 entitled *Hygiasticion* (*A Plea for Sobriety*) concerning the preservation of life and health to extreme old age. Lessius, in his book, amplified Cornaro's theories as a means to enjoy good health.

Fast forward about three hundred years from Lessius, and we find the American inventor, Thomas Edison, who, like Lessius, was also a fan of Cornaro and his essays. Edison followed the guidelines of Cornaro, but unlike Cornaro, as he grew older, Edison continued to reduce the quantity of his food to the point that he only drank milk. This may or may not have extended his life, but he did continue to work to create new inventions throughout his life, dying at age eighty-four.

Another means which has been touted to enjoy good health through our diet, but unlike Cornaro, is by the reduction of meat in one's diet. John Harvey Kellogg, who, along with his brother, invented the cornflakes breakfast cereal, strictly believed in a meatless diet. Kellogg was a medical doctor who was born before the Civil War and lived to see World War II. He practiced medicine in both Michigan and Florida during his career. Among his clientele were Amelia Earhart and Henry Ford. Kellogg advocated that in order to stay healthy, one must restrict his diet to vegetables, along with wholesome products like fruit and nuts. Kellogg also recognized that fats in food could cause health problems, which correlates with our information today regarding cholesterol. He believed that eating meat was one of the main causes of health problems and disease and contended that our simian ancestors were vegetarians, and that meat was not necessary for one's diet. To support his claim, Kellogg asserted that the ancient wrestler Milo of Croton, who won the Olympic games six times, was a vegetarian. By following his own advice, Kellogg, even though he only had one lung and had health problems early in life, lived into his nineties.

Like Kellogg, Sylvester Graham, the founder of Graham crackers, was also a vegetarian. In 1837, he published *Treatise on Bread and Breadmaking* and advocated a diet of vegetables and bran. Thousands of Americans would become vegetarians as a result of Graham's treatise. Graham Societies were formed throughout the United States which supported his teachings. He blamed diseases on fried meats, alcohol, and eating too fast. Emerson called him the "poet of bran, bread, and muffins".

In fact, today, there are many who believe that vegetarianism is the way to preserve health and gain longevity. Even former President Bill Clinton has gone from eating "Big Macs" and other "fast-food" to only eating fruits, vegetables, and beans. He claims that he is now a full fledged vegan.

While many touted the way to good health was through vegetarianism, Dr. Ancel Keys asserted that the best means of preserving health through our diet is by what he termed as "The Mediterranean Diet". Dr. Keys, who earned two doctorates - one in biology and one in physiology - conducted a study of men living in Italy, the Greek Islands, Yugoslavia, the Netherlands, Finland, Japan, and the United States. The results of the study found that saturated fats may be the cause of arterial blockage which could cause heart attacks. The study resulted in a book in 1980 entitled "The Mediterranean Diet". Even though the diet derived more than 35% of its calories from fat, it supported a diet rich in fruits, vegetables, pasta, bread and olive oil, with meat, fish, and dairy products used as condiments. Dr. Keys, with his wife, wrote two other best selling books, *Eat Well and Stay Well* and *How to Eat Well and Stay Well the Mediterranean Way*. Assuming he lived by his own recipes, Dr. Keys' diet appears to have worked well for him, for he lived to be 100.

When it comes to diet, Mahatma Gandhi believed that fasting was the best means to preserve one's health. Gandhi said that to stay healthy and to live as long as you can, you need to fast: "Fast - if you are constipated, if you are anemic, if you are feverish, if you have indigestion, if you have a headache, if you are rheumatic, if you are gouty, if you are fretting and foaming, if you are depressed." He said to do this, you will avoid having to take any medicine. Fasting not only seemed to work for Gandhi's health, but it was also used by him as a political tool to obtain India's independence from British rule.

I could have continued forever studying diets, for there appears to be no shortage of them. In fact, there are thousands of diets, such as "The 5-second Flat Belly Secret Diet", the "Mayo Clinic Diet", the "Crazy Sexy Diet", and "The Ultimate Diet Guide". Like the recipes for longevity, there are diets of every kind and character, but I was satisfied so far with my research that diet may have a direct relationship to health and longevity.

In my study of health, I next delved into exercise. Prior to 1960, much of our exercise was obtained through normal daily activities, rather than a forced regimen at the gym or otherwise. For example, growing up in a small town, I watched businessmen walk to work, and it was common for me to walk and ride my bicycle to school and all over town. Today, we ride in a car everywhere. The average housewife in the past was cleaning and dusting, whereas today modern conveniences such as dryers for clothes now keep us from stretching to put clothes on the line. Lawns were mowed with push mowers. Now, we ride. Today, we can watch television and even change the channels without moving from our chair. These modern conveniences are wonderful, but it appears they are not necessarily wonderful for our health.

Delving into the past, in order to maintain good health and prolong one's life, many of the ancients were great believers in exercise to maintain their health. The Greeks had gymnasiums for exercise, and the Spartans particularly believed in exercising profusely as a way of life, and the Olympics, of course, are an outgrowth of the Greeks and their way of life. The Romans, too, had gymnasiums for exercise and believed that regular bathing was also good for their health.

Benjamin Franklin addressed exercise in the 18th century. Franklin touted walking and the use of the dumb bell for exercise. Franklin said, "there is more exercise in one mile riding on horseback than five in a coach, and more in walking one mile on foot than five on horseback... there is more in walking one mile up and down stairs than in five on a level floor."

The third President of the United States, John Adams, also addressed the importance of exercise when he said, "Move or die is the language of our Maker in the constitution of our bodies. One must rouse oneself from lethargy. When you cannot walk abroad, walk in your room." Adams purportedly walked several miles each day.

The necessity for exercise, in more recent times, was addressed by Dr. Jeremy Morris, a British epidemiologist. He reviewed physical activities as they related to heart problems in the middle of the 20th century. During his career, Dr. Morris used the famous British double-decker buses as a means to prove that heart attacks may be prevented by physical activity. He studied the drivers who sat and drove ninety percent of their working day versus the conductors who climbed up and down the stairs of the buses an average of 600 stairs each day. He found that the conductors who were constantly exercising had less than half of the heart attacks as the drivers who seldom moved around the bus. In addition, he used postal workers for another study, comparing those who delivered the mail by walking or riding bicycles with the postal clerks who only maintained the windows at the post office. He found similar results as with the conductors and bus drivers. Dr. Morris, himself, began exercising in early childhood and continued throughout his life by swimming, biking, or walking at least half an hour each day. He would live to reach 99 ½ years of age.

It appears that exercise is not just good for the physical body, but may be good for the brain as well. My quest into health subjects shows that brain-related problems, such as Alzheimer's and dementia, may be less in people who are physically active. In fact, physical activity dropped dementia risks for people who were only somewhat physically active, but the risk substantially dropped for dementia related problems for those who were much more physically active and exercised. In addition to physical exercise, mental exercises such as working crossword puzzles, reading, writing, traveling, taking classes, playing board games or card games appears to substantially reduce dementia and memory loss as one ages.

As to the other elements of what I deemed healthy practices, I knew smoking was bad for you, and of course, one should be temperate with alcohol, one should get a good night's sleep, and good hygiene should be a must. Therefore, I did not make these a major part of my research. I had now covered diet and exercise and their histories and how they affect our health and longevity, so I now began to focus more on individual's lives and their health habits.

Among those I studied was the painter Georgia O'Keefe, who seemed to stay young all of her life. She maintained an extremely healthy lifestyle. She arose every morning at dawn and performed a series of exercises and walked the hills around her home. She also raised her own organic food in her garden and would freeze and store pickles and can her own vegetables. She drank tea and watched her diet carefully, all of which presumably enabled her to have the energy and vitality for her art until she died at age ninety-eight.

Two of the seemingly healthiest and certainly the strongest people I encountered in my research were Angelo Siciliano and Jack LaLanne. Siciliano, who was born in Italy, came to America through Ellis Isle as a youngster and grew up in Brooklyn in the early 1900's. In his youth, he was a ninety-eight pound weakling, but after a bully kicked sand in his face on the beach one day, Siciliano realized that he must do something to become healthier and stronger. He couldn't afford weights so he studied lions at the zoo and noticed how they were always in superb physical shape, even though they were caged. He recognized what kept the lions physically strong was the way they stretched, and thus, he developed a program of exercising which he called dynamic tension. By using this program and other health remedies such as a healthy diet, aerobic exercise, and no smoking or drinking, Angelo Siciliano transformed himself into a "Hercules" of the 20th century and changed his name to Charles Atlas. He was so strong that he tore thick phone books in half, bent iron bars, and even once pulled a 145,000 pound train. His success resulted with him being crowned the "World's Most Perfectly Developed Man", and he started a mail-order fitness course explaining his method of exercising which was sold to millions world-wide.

Like Siciliano, Jack LaLanne described himself as an emotional and physical wreck in his youth, but, at age fifteen, he turned his life around with good health practices which continued the remainder of his life. He became a national fitness guru, having his own television show, "The Jack LaLanne Show" which ran for more than twenty years. At sixty, he swam from Alcatraz Island to Fisherman's Wharf handcuffed, shackled, and towing a 1,000 pound boat. At seventy, handcuffed and shackled again, he towed seventy boats, carrying a total of seventy people, a mile and a half through Long Beach Harbor. To keep healthy, LaLanne, who claimed "exercise was king and nutrition was queen" maintained a diet which consisted of two meals a day, and the shunning of snacks. His breakfast usually consisted of hard-boiled egg whites, broth, oatmeal with soy milk and fruit. His other meal was usually a salad made of raw vegetables and egg whites along with fish and a mixture of red and white wine. Occasionally, he would allow himself a roast turkey sandwich, but he never drank coffee. In addition to his diet, he worked out each day. As a result of their lifestyles, both Atlas and LaLanne found health, strength, fame, and financial reward.

Even today, there are those who are pursuing what they believe to be a healthy lifestyle. One of those is Jane Fonda, who, in her seventies, says that she maintains a strict diet so she can continue to hike, swim, and do other sports. Her diet consists of "zero trans fats, zero partially hydrogenated oils" and "no desserts, period". On her daily menu: lots of grilled or steamed fish and chicken, fresh fruit and vegetables (especially dark green), dairy and the occasional piece of lean, red bison meat. According to Fonda, this has kept her cholesterol and blood pressure low. In addition, she exercises by walking and riding an exercise bike at least four days a week. She also works out with weights and practices yoga, and she makes sure she gets plenty of sleep each night. However, she does confess that aging has had an effect on her life in that she reveals that she has osteoarthritis and osteoporosis, takes a number of medications, and has had knee and hip replacements.

Things seemed to be going well on my study of health. It appeared that if you lived a healthy life, you could maintain your health, be strong, and live a long life; and that only the abuse or neglect of our bodies (such as overeating, lack of exercise, use of tobacco, and abuse of alcohol) would be the causes which would shorten life and result in growing old as my father did.

However, as I continued, this did not necessarily seem to be the case. For example, when considering exercise, Jim Fixx, who basically started the jogging craze of the 1970's and wrote *The Complete Book of Running,* died while on his daily run at the age of fifty-two. Also, Dr. Lynn Smaha, a heart specialist and a former President of the American Heart Association who was also a runner, died in 2006 of a heart attack after exercising at age sixty-three. And I recall the former Governor of Florida, Lawton Chiles, dying in 1998 in the Governor's Mansion's gymnasium next to his cycling machine. I even remembered that one of my college professors dropped dead while unlacing his running shoes after a morning jog.

Moreover, considering diet, I recall J. I. Rodale, who promoted a healthy and active lifestyle by eating organic food which he claimed would prevent disease and give one longevity. However, only minutes after boasting that he was in excellent health, claiming that he would live to be 100 while appearing as a guest on *The Dick Cavett Show,* Rodale would slump over dead at the age of seventy-two of a heart attack. And Linda McCartney, who ate no meat, died of cancer at fifty-six. In addition, I started recalling friends who seemed to have done everything possible to live a long life by using all of the proper health practices, and yet wound up with Alzheimer's, cancer, or heart trouble.

Then, as I delved further into my biographies, I learned of many who did not necessarily follow the rules of good health practices, but yet lived as long or longer than those who did live the healthy life. For instance, when I studied John Adams, he appeared to focus on his health in his latter years by exercising and maintaining a proper diet. He maintained that vegetables should be the main diet with little animal food and still less "spiritous liquors". Yet I learned that each morning to get his day started, he drank a "tankard" of hard cider (an alcoholic drink). Also,

I found that the Adams' family's meals may have consisted of turkeys, roast beef, veal, bacon, mutton, vegetables, Indian pudding, molasses, butter, pies, and tarts. Furthermore, he continuously smoked cigars to the point that it worried his wife, Abigail. Also, Adams did not appear to get enough rest, for he was always reading, studying, and writing well into the nights. Yet he never grew old and had the energy and mental alertness of a man half his age right up until his death at ninety.

Like Adams, Winston Churchill, maintained vigor and vitality throughout his life. He was a prolific writer, historian, politician, statesman, and artist. At age sixty-four, at a time when most men are retiring, he became Prime Minister of England for the first time and served for five years throughout World War II. During the war, he would rally his countrymen with his speeches and his youthful energy, travelling over 100,000 miles, sometimes through hostile skies. When the war ended, his tenure as Prime Minister also ended, but this did not put an end to Churchill's political life. Rather than retire, Churchill, when he reached the age of seventy-seven, again led his party and served England as Prime Minister, continuing to serve until he was eighty-one. Even afterwards, he still remained a member of Parliament and continued to be extremely active in all realms of life until his death at age ninety. One would believe as long and full a life as Churchill led, that he would have followed all of the regimens recommended for proper health. However, instead, Churchill maintained a portly figure and very seldom exercised. His normal daily routine could consist of breakfast of steak, smoked herring fried in butter, eggs, roast beef, kidneys, bacon, sausage, porridge, toast, butter, marmalade, jam, tea with milk, and orange juice. He would remain in bed until late in the morning and usually took two hot baths a day and a two hour nap in the afternoon. After breakfast, he would start his alcohol intake with a scotch and soda cocktail. In fact, alcohol was in his body twenty-four hours a day. In the course of a day, he would have as many as three scotches, two brandies, and several glasses of champagne. In addition, Churchill smoked cigars all day long. At lunch, he often had Irish stew, Yorkshire pudding with roast beef, and more alcohol, such as brandy and port. In the evening, his dinner could consist of wine, soup, oysters, caviar, cheese, pate, trout, lamb, lobster, crab, scampi, sole, chocolate eclairs, roast beef, Yorkshire pudding, and more port and brandy. Then he would have more cigars after dinner. So what kept Churchill going so long with so much energy, while living this unhealthy lifestyle? The answer was illusive.

Even Benjamin Franklin, who had the energy and youthfulness of a thirty year old throughout his life, may have violated the rules. In fact, his life may have been a paradox, for Franklin once wrote, "To lengthen thy life, lesson thy meals." However, it appears that he did not live by his own advice. Franklin would maintain his stocky frame by having breakfast usually at eight o'clock on week days and later on Sundays. This meal may consist of bread and butter, honey, and coffee or hot chocolate. For dinner he could have hors d'oeuvres, followed with beef, veal, mutton, or fowl, some vegetables, plus candies and pastry, biscuits, butter, and pickles. Like Churchill, Franklin also enjoyed the pleasures of life, for John Adams noted that while both he and Franklin were in France, Franklin regularly attended the salons in Paris and was always sipping champagne. And he must have enjoyed other spirits for Franklin's cellar, at one time, held over one thousand bottles of wine and many bottles of rum. Even though he touted exercise as a way to maintain good health, I never read much that indicated to me that Franklin exercised regularly in his latter years. Yet with this diet of food, drink, and lifestyle, Franklin still lived a long life with unbelievable vitality.

One of the most interesting people I studied who lived a long life and continued working at his craft until the end of his life (but who didn't follow the regimens of health and exercise) was Michelangelo, known for painting the ceiling of the Sistine Chapel in Rome. His hygiene was terrible in that he seldom washed. Though he was rich, he lived as a poor man, not following any dietary rules whatsoever, eating whatever was available, sometimes only left-over bread. For exercise, he said the use of his hammer and chisel was enough. He was even lazy at times, for he would sleep with his clothes on, keeping his boots on too, for he maintained that why should he take off his boots when he was going to have to put them back on the next day anyway. In fact, he would wear his boots at times for so long that his skin would come off when he did remove them. Even though he lived this unhealthy lifestyle, he would still live, produce, and create until his death at age eighty-eight, at a time when forty was old.

If anyone abused the rules of health throughout his life, it was Bertrand Russell, the accomplished British author, philosopher, and critic, who lived an extremely active life throughout his life. Russell once made this statement: "When I was young I was told that smoking would shorten my life. After sixty years of smoking, it hasn't shortened much - anyway I get much more pleasure from smoking than I would from a few more years in decrepitude. I smoke heavily and only stop to sleep or eat.... I'll die if I can't smoke." In fact, he even justified his smoking by describing that smoking had actually saved him from death.

Russell was in a plane crash and at the time of the crash, he was in the smoking section of the airplane because of his habit. He was not killed, but all of the passengers in the non-smoking compartment died. Aside from smoking, Russell made it clear that he had never worked at doing anything that may be good for his health. He said he ate and drank what he liked, which included whiskey, and he believed that the best way to keep your health was to forget about yourself. Even though Russell lived what many would believe an unhealthy lifestyle, he would live fully and vigorously. At seventy-nine, he was writing his autobiography; at eighty, he was working twelve hours a day; at eighty-nine, he was campaigning against nuclear arms which even brought him a jail sentence; and only two days before his death at age ninety-seven, he was still politically active, taking a stance on Mideast problems.

Like Russell, the best-selling author Barbara Holland, was so opposed to the so-called healthy life that she wrote a collection of essays entitled *Endangered Pleasures: In Defense of Naps, Bacon, Martinis, Profanity, and Other Indulgences,* describing her views on health and life. She touted smoking, along with drinking, as pleasures in life, and said that, "I was sick and tired of being lectured by dear friends with their little bottles of water and their regular visits to the gym." She declared that, "I'm not really in favor of health and fitness." Yet, she kept her vitality even under these circumstances, and at the age of seventy-two, wrote a best-seller memoir entitled, *When All the World Was Young.*

Another who violated the rules of health was the columnist Irv Kupcinet's wife of sixty-two years, Essee. She loved tobacco so much that she was buried with two packs of unfiltered Pall Mall cigarettes. In addition,

Chauncey Depew, a lawyer, businessman, and public official in the late 1800's and early 1900's, lived to be ninety-four at a time when life expectancy was not very long. When asked about his exercise regimen to attain good health and long life, Depew chimed, "I get my exercise acting as pallbearer to my friends who exercise."

Moreover, as I plodded through my books, my material, and my thoughts, I began to be confused for it seemed that for every person that I found who lived a long and energetic life by using good health practices, I would find another person who seemed to defy good health practices and yet lived as long, if not longer, still with a youthful outlook on life. For instance, the strong and healthy Charles Atlas would die at eighty, whereas the portly and health abuser Winston Churchill died at ninety. The muscle-man Jack LaLanne would live to be ninety-six living an extremely healthy life, but was outlived by the pipe-smoker Bertrand Russell who died at ninety-seven, living an extremely unhealthy life. Bear in mind, in his nineties, Russell still had the vitality of a man half his age. Along these same lines, the founder of "Graham crackers" Sylvester Graham who touted vegetarianism as the way to health and longevity, only lived into his fifties, whereas I learned of a lady named Gertrude Baines, who included as her favorite foods, fried chicken, bacon, and ice cream, and lived to be one of the oldest recorded persons, dying at 115. Even our mountain-climber "Grandma Whitney" claimed she had violated her own health rules by jogging when she should have walked. She was right, for the famous Olympic runner, Jesse Owens, spoke on this subject when he said that no one over sixty should be out there jogging.

Then I recalled from my hometown my old friend,

Mary. Thinking of Mary reminded me of the ancient Greek Diogenes, who lived during the time of Alexander the Great. Even though they lived hundreds of years apart, they seemed to have a lot in common. Diogenes wore rags for clothes, whereas Mary wore clothes in the 1960's that were apparently from the thirties. Diogenes slept in a barrel in Athens, whereas Mary slept in a chair in the courthouse. Neither lived a healthy life, neither ate well; Diogenes begged for his food. While Mary did not beg for her food, she could eat on a "York Peppermint Pattie" for a whole day. I don't know whether Diogenes had any vices, but Mary smoked all of her life. Both were brilliant; Diogenes was a philosopher, and Mary, in her own way, was a philosopher and helped with research in the courthouse. They were both always learning and both were curious; both appeared to be happy, but neither probably bathed often. Both had a positive attitude; in fact, Mary would talk with anyone. Diogenes was so positive with his attitude that he once told Alexander the Great (who would conquer the known world) to move out of his way for he was blocking his sunlight. Yet, living these unhealthy lifestyles, both Diogenes and Mary would live extra-ordinary long lives. Diogenes lived into his 90th year, and Mary, whom I knew to be ancient at the time of her death, but, like a lot of women, never revealed her age to me.

I'm also reminded of a friend who at eighty-five, was still practicing law; it is claimed that he can't die because the Environmental Protection Agency will not allow his body to be placed in the soil due to the enormous amounts of alcohol and cigarettes he's consumed throughout his life. But in his 86th year, he has a purpose in life - the practice of law, and he faithfully dons his clothes each morning and heads to the office.

Then there is the bluesman Pinetop Perkins, who loved cheeseburgers and didn't give up drinking until he was eighty-two, having smoked since the age of nine, won Grammys for blues albums, one at the age of ninety-four and another at ninety-seven. A centenarian, Milton Garland, who at age 102, when asked if he had a special diet, he said, "I eat anything but sauerkraut."

As I pondered on these confusing issues, I realized that even the experts don't seem to agree about some of these matters. For instance, jogging can be considered good for you; however, a new study shows that excessive endurance exercise can lead to the development of scarring of areas of the heart and cause abnormal heart rhythms which may increase coronary heart disease. Eggs used to be bad for you, now they're not so bad. Coffee was certainly considered bad for you at one time; however, in 2011, a new study indicated that coffee may actually be good for you in that it may lower the risk of prostate cancer for it appears that men who drank at least six cups a day had a sixty percent reduction for the aggressive type of prostate cancer. Even men who drank only three cups a day had a thirty percent chance of getting the deadliest type of prostate cancer. In fact, it has been found that coffee may reduce the risk of diabetes, liver disease, and Parkinson's disease, and even women who drink at least five cups a day have nearly a sixty percent lower risk of aggressive breast cancer which doesn't respond to estrogen. Also, another recent study indicates that drinking coffee may help you live longer. And although I knew that a good night's sleep should be good for you, another study points out that if you snore, your risk of cancer is increased five-fold. Thus, there must be something else that gave Churchill, Russell, Pinetop Perkins, and others this longevity, and in particular, their youthful outlook on life and their vitality that they had throughout their entire lives besides just good health practices. It was hard for me to believe that merely genetics kept them alive so long. In fact, there has been a recent study which involved almost five hundred people between the ages of 95 and 109, comparing them with over three thousand others born during the same period. The results of the study revealed that longevity may not be from a healthy life at all, for many who drank, smoked, ate unhealthily, and took little exercise, still lived extremely long lives. This, along with all of the various recipes I found that people gave as their secret to their extra-ordinary longevity, made my situation more confusing than ever.

Thus, I began to realize that my focus needed to be on what all of these people who stayed young had in common, rather than how their lifestyles were different, for it appeared to me that many, regardless of whether they were health conscious or not, never grew old. It became obvious that many of the people I had encountered had found something else to keep them from growing old, whether they lived a healthy life or not. It became clear to me while the healthy life may make us feel better, it won't necessarily give us longevity or keep us from growing old.

As time went by, my thoughts regarding longevity also began to change as they had regarding a healthy lifestyle. As I visited my ninety-three year old mother in a nursing home (who may or may not have realized who I was), as I periodically attended funerals of friends who had passed away, and as I re-thought through all of the material I had gathered, I realized that my research needed to change directions once again, for I began to see that it was not *how long* we may live that matters (even though living as long as you can is a worthy goal) but what is *more* important, is *how* we live, so not to grow old as my father did.

CHAPTER 6

SEARCHING FOR THE FOUNTAIN OF YOUTH

"Everyone is the age he has decided on,
and I've decided on 30."
Pablo Picasso, in his 80's

After changing my direction from longevity and health to never growing old, I still continued my daily routine of collecting data, and I kept reading biographies and other books for I needed to find others who stayed young in order for me to fully learn what they had that my father didn't. In other words, I was looking for the secret to the "fountain of youth".

Since the beginning of time man has tried to discover how to retain youth to keep from growing old. Throughout history, many attempts have been made, including one by the ancient Greeks. They believed that if a man slept between two young girls for a period of time, his youth would be restored from the breath of the maidens. Of course, this did not succeed. Another in history that also attempted to retain youth was Charles E. Brown-Sequard, a 19th century physician and physiologist of the College de France, who believed he had found a way to stay young by injecting himself with a glandular extract that he had created. He performed his experiments on himself at age seventy-one, but, like the Greeks, his mission failed, and he died five years later.

One of the most bizarre cases of an attempt to retain youth is the story of Countess Elizabeth Bathory of Hungary, who lived in the late 16th and early 17th century.

The Countess sought to retain youth so desperately that over a twenty year period, she tortured and killed as many as six hundred girls and young women, using their blood to bathe in, which she believed would allow her to retain her beauty and youth. Unfortunately for the Countess, her crimes would be discovered, and she would be tried and convicted. And, of course, she would also die.

Another bizarre method used to attempt to retain youth was through the use of elixirs. Elixirs arose out of the practice of alchemy, which is associated with turning common metals into gold. This practice is traceable back to ancient Egypt and was considered a serious science in Europe up until the 16th century. It was believed throughout this period that man could make a potion or drink which was created from gold or other like substances that supposedly would cure all diseases, prolong life indefinitely, and grant the drinker eternal youth. It was referred to as "the elixir of life". In ancient China, various emperors also sought the fabled elixir. However, rather than gold, the Chinese concentrated on ingesting long-lasting precious substances, such as jade, cinebar, or hematite. The practice of alchemy and the use of elixirs faded from existence because like other attempts to retain youth, they failed.

I had my own experience with a possible elixir of life. Long before there was a Disney World, there was a Florida of many varied vacation attractions. Families poured into Florida each year to see the Everglades with its alligators, the ocean at Miami Beach, Cypress Gardens, and Silver Springs, with its glass bottom boats. When I was about seven years old, my family took one of these vacations. One particular sight still fresh in my memory was going to the spring which was said to have been the flowing waters of the "fountain of youth". Our tour guide assured us that this was the very spring from which legend held that the Spanish Explorer Ponce de Leon had found. As I remember, our host said Ponce de Leon had come to the New World with Christopher Columbus on his second voyage in 1493. Our tour guide continued to reveal the story of Ponce de Leon who conquered what is now Puerto Rico for Spain and became its Governor. The guide told us that while Ponce de Leon was Governor, he learned of a tale from the Indians of an island to the north, which had a spring that contained waters which would restore youth. Intrigued by these stories, Ponce de Leon, at the age of fifty-three, set out to discover the location of the wonder giving waters. As we all know, there was no "fountain of youth" that flowed from the spring. In fact, Ponce de Leon was to die a short eight years afterward, disappointed, and "old at heart".

However, our tour guide held us spell-bound as he further related the story of Ponce de Leon and enticed us with hope that a drink from the spring may yet provide us with the magical results that Ponce de Leon did not find. Each visitor was then presented with a small paper cup filled with water allowing us to drink the magical waters from the spring. The water was cool and refreshing on that hot summer day. But, like Ponce de Leon, no member of my family, especially my father, found eternal youth from the spring. Regardless, the stories of Ponce de Leon and the fountain of youth have not discouraged, and will not discourage, others from continuing to seek what Ponce de Leon sought, and it is happening every day around us and will probably continue throughout the history of mankind.

Even the construction or renovation of buildings, poems, books, and paintings have been used in an attempt to stop the aging process. For instance, Arakawa, a Japanese-born artist and designer who lived in New York, touted that aging could be outlawed; he lived by a philosophy called *Reversible Destiny.* Through this philosophy, he created buildings and art which he believed would stop aging and even prevent death. But like the others, this did not keep him young or prevent his own death which occurred in 2010 at the age of seventy-three.

In an attempt to stop the aging process, the corporate executive, Sumner Redstone, who along with his family owns CBS, Viacom, and MTV networks, at eighty-four years of age, said that he planned to live another fifty years. His secret is the elixir, MonaVie, which is an antioxidant-rich mixture, of which the main ingredient is produced from the Brazilian Acai berry. Redstone, as a result of his regular doses of the mixture, claimed that he looked younger than he was, and that he felt only forty years old. He said that it is a miracle drug. Maybe he has found the fountain of youth, but, only time will tell.

Today even modern medicine has joined the ranks searching for the secret to the fountain of youth. Billions of dollars are being spent for cosmetic surgery in an effort to slow down or reverse the aging process. In fact, in the last twelve years, the number of cosmetic surgeries performed in the United States have rapidly increased at an unbelievable rate for both American women and men. From 1997 to 2007, the total number of cosmetic procedures performed rose 457%. I predict that these "fountain of youth" procedures will continue to accelerate even more in that 54 million Americans will turn sixty-five years or older by the year 2020. The procedures range from tummy tucks to face-lifts, and recently, I read about an eighty-three year old great-grandmother who made national headlines by spending $8,000.00 for a three hour procedure just to boost her breasts. Plastic surgery clinics are performing breast surgery, body contouring, liposuction, facial surgery, chemical peels, facials and waxing, microdermabrasion, eyelash and brow tinting, and body treatments. In addition to the cutting, carving, and stitching, the needle has also become a major means to attempt to preserve youth. Most of us are familiar with botox in which a needle is stuck into the forehead and other parts of the face to remove wrinkles, and now, there is a human growth hormone that is being utilized by many celebrities. This hormone has been available for over ten years, but it has recently been re-introduced as an anti-aging drug. Users are paying up to $240.00 per injection for these chemicals, even with the increased risk of cancer, diabetes, and heart disease; but they claim that it makes them feel twenty years younger.

Now we see anti-aging clinics sprouting up throughout the United States, as well as anti-aging products which are being sold that promise youth; in fact, the anti-aging industry is now a $50 billion a year business, selling creams, lotions, and other anti-aging products. But, like Ponce de Leon, Dr. Sequard, Arakawa, Countess Bathory, and I'm sure many others, like them, are looking in the wrong places to stay young.

As our population ages, there will probably be many more people to go for the quick fix of procedures to retain youth, but what they must realize is that as the name implies, it will only be *cosmetic.* These surgeries and treatments are changing appearances, and many people may feel better about themselves as a result. In fact, a friend of mine once told me that he believed that every person has a duty to look as nice as they can. I do not argue with that; in fact, I agree that we should. So if a facelift or a little botox makes you feel better or look nicer, have at it. But from what I've learned, it will not keep you young. It will be like a false idol that you will be worshiping. What is so sad is that many who have had these procedures may not have even needed them, for some of the most beautiful women I've seen have never had a facelift. This, I attribute to their inner beauty which makes its way to the outside. And as for men, many become more handsome as they grow older, and gray hair and a certain amount of wrinkles actually enhance their features. What is even worse are those who have had facelifts resulting in no wrinkles in their face, but in their place, a freak appears — a stretched, unnatural stiff face has replaced a beautiful wrinkled one.

But what surprised me is that when I delved into history, there is nothing new about this subject, for the poet Martial who was born in Spain in 40 A.D. wrote the following poem almost two thousand years ago:

An Old Dandy
You wish, Laetinus, to be thought a youth,
And so you dye your hair.
You're suddenly a crow, forsooth:
Of late a swan you were!
You can't cheat all: there is a Lady dread
Who knows your hair is grey:
Proserpina will pounce upon your head,
And tear the mask away.

So as I pondered these things, I asked the question: If youth is not found in the carving of our bodies or through medical tricks or other procedures which may make us look somewhat younger on the outside, then where is it found? I now knew that regardless of one's lifestyle, whether

84

healthy like our mountain-climbing lady Hulda Crooks, or unhealthy, such as Churchill, that it was possible to stay young all of one's life. But I still needed to find a consensus – enough people who had found youth to give me sufficient information to find the answer to my question. Thus, I wondered, who else had found ways to stay young all of their lives? And what was their secret? How were they able to stay young right up to their deaths, regardless of how they old they became?

As I mentioned earlier, even though Benjamin Franklin's lifestyle may have been a paradox, it was obvious that he had found what I termed as the "fountain of youth". When Franklin was eighty-two years old, he was the oldest man at the Continental Congress in 1775. William Pierce of Georgia who observed Franklin at this time said that Franklin possessed "an activity of mind equal to the youth of 25 years of age". Also, two years later, Dr. Manasseh Cutler, a clergyman from Massachusetts, had an occasion to study Franklin and described him accordingly, "I was highly delighted with the extensive knowledge he appeared to have of every subject, the brightness of his memory, and clearness and vivacity of all his mental faculties, notwithstanding his age (eight-four)." Cutler went on to describe Franklin that he had "an incessant vein of humour, accompanied with an uncommon vivacity, which seems as natural and involuntary as his breathing."

And like Franklin, I knew that Albert Einstein must have discovered the way to stay young for he said, "People like me... never grow old. We never cease to stand like curious children before the great mystery into which we were born." Also, Socrates must have found it — for he was taking dancing lessons at age seventy. Julia Child surely found it, for she was still traveling the world cooking and

85

making plans for a new TV series, still young at the age of eighty-six. The actress, Beah Richards, discovered youth also for she was still acting at the age of eighty, winning an Emmy award for her performance in the TV drama, "The Practice". The baseball player, Branch Rickey, in describing his father, made it clear that his father had discovered the "fountain of youth". He said, "My father was 86 when he died. As an old man, he was still planting peach and apple trees on our farm – who would take in the fruit was not important to him."

So I continued to look, and I learned of many others who found the way to stay young. One was Helene Bertha Amalie Riefenstahl, known as "Leni", who was born in 1902 in Berlin, Germany. Leni would grow up in a financially well-off family, and early in life, she would discover a love for the performing arts. She became a successful dancer, actress, a well-known director and was known throughout Europe. She would be called by some as the most successful woman film maker of the 20th century. When Adolf Hitler rose to power, Leni aligned herself with the Nazi Party and Hitler. Although she claimed she was never a member of the Nazi Party, she did make films for the Third Reich. This relationship with Hitler and his Party would haunt her and her career for the rest of her life. Her film career as a director and actress was ruined by her Nazi background. However, Leni did not let this problem stop her from leading a full and successful life until the day she died at 101. At the age of sixty, Leni, having totally failed at attempting to revive her career in films, did not give up; she chose a new career and took up photography. She first began a study of a remote Nubi Tribe in Sudan, Africa. She would learn their language and photograph their people. Afterwards, at age seventy, she would have the opportunity to underwater dive and snorkel in the Indian Ocean. Enthralled by this experience, Leni would lie about her age claiming she was fifty-two in order to be certified for scuba diving. Successful in this endeavor, she began a new career of underwater photography. At seventy-two, she continued her contact with the Nubi Tribe and was even granted a Sudanese citizenship. She would also locate another Sudanese tribe, which was even more remote than the Nubi Tribe. At age seventy-three, Leni won the Gold Medal of Art Directors Club of Germany for "Best Photo Achievement of the Year". Also, she continued her underwater photography - this time she would photograph underwater in the Red Sea. At age seventy-six, she published two volumes of her underwater photos. At age eighty-two, she published two books of photography of Africa. At age eighty-eight, she published another photography book, *Underwater Waters*. At age ninety-five, Leni was adding an addition to her home to handle future projects that she had planned regarding her photography. At age ninety-seven, she traveled again to Sudan during a Civil War. At age ninety-nine, she edited and produced a film "Impressions Underwater" which was released on her 100th birthday. At 100, Leni was still young and was still diving.

Another who found youth was the American baseball player and manager, Cornelius McGillicuddy, Sr., also known as "Connie Mack". Born in 1862 to a poor family, he left school at the age of fourteen and would later become the longest-serving manager in Major League Baseball history. As manager of the Philadelphia Athletics for fifty baseball seasons, the Athletics would win the World Series five times. Connie Mack, like Leni, found youth and lived life to its fullest. At age sixty-seven, Connie Mack would lead the Philadelphia Athletics to win the World Series for the fourth time. At age sixty-eight, he would once again lead his team to win the World Series for the fifth time. At age seventy-two, Mr. Mack took a group of All-Star baseball players to Japan for exhibition games for the Japanese people who loved baseball; his entourage included Babe Ruth and Lou Gehrig. At age seventy-five, Connie Mack was elected to the Hall of Fame. Even at age seventy-eight, after a long illness which affected Mack and his team, Mack would bounce back and rebuild the team. With this youthful energy, he was awarded an honorary Ph.D., and at the age of seventy-nine was voted "#1 Sportsman of 1941". At age eighty-five, he celebrated his 64th year in baseball. During these years, his Philadelphia Athletics had drawn over two million fans at home and on the road. At age eighty-seven, the energy was still there. Connie Mack was still managing his team. When asked about retiring, he said he was having too much fun to retire. At age eighty-nine, he wrote *My 66 Years in Baseball*. Connie Mack would die young at age ninety-three.

Also among those who found youth was William James Durant who was born in North Adams, Massachusetts in 1885. He was a lecturer, teacher, philosopher, historian, and writer. He received his doctorate in 1917. In 1926 he published *The Story of Philosophy* which became a best-seller earning him enough money to give him financial independence. It was at this point in his life that he decided to formulate a purpose for his life which was to write the history of mankind which he called *The Story of Civilization*, which I have referred to earlier. The project began in 1927 and did not end until 1975; his history resulted in eleven volumes consisting of a total of 9,941 pages. The first volume was *Our Oriental Heritage,* and the last volume was *The Age of Napoleon. The Story of Civilization* covered one hundred and ten centuries of human history. To write this series of books, Durant made it a point to go to the original source for his research. This entailed eight trips to Europe and two trips around the world. Even though his project would take almost fifty years, he still found time to write other books. When Will Durant was sixty-eight years old, he had finished four volumes of *The Story of Civilization* and was publishing the fifth volume, *The Renaissance*. In addition, he published another book, not in the series, called *The Pleasures of Philosophy*. With undaunted energy, at age seventy-six, Durant, along with his wife, Ariel, wrote and published *The Age of Reason Begins*. At age eighty, he and his wife published *The Age of Voltaire.* Never stopping in his pursuit to fulfill his mission, at age eighty-two, Durant along with his wife began writing another book called *The Lessons of History* which would be published when he was eighty-three, and at the same time, they also published in the *Civilization* series, *Rousseau and the Revolution,* which would win the Pulitzer Prize. At age eighty-five, Durant and Ariel would publish another book not in the series entitled *Interpretations of Life*, but they also continued to write the next volume in their series, *The Age of Napoleon*. This book of the series would take four years to complete and not be published until Durant was ninety. At age ninety-two, Durant and Ariel published their autobiography, *A Dual Biography*. Never tiring, that same year, Durant would begin an audio series called *Heroes of History*. His work would bring him the Medal of Freedom, the highest honor bestowed on a civilian in the United States. Will Durant would continue to write and produce history and philosophy books until his death. He died young at ninety-six.

I knew Georgia O'Keefe had lived the healthy life, but I wanted to know more about her since I believed that she had also discovered the "fountain of youth". Ms. O'Keefe was born in 1887 in Sun Prairie, Wisconsin. Her family would move to Virginia where she would graduate from high school and afterwards attend the Art Institute of Chicago. She would later live in Texas, becoming an elementary school art teacher and thereafter, a college art teacher. She would eventually move to New York City and marry Alfred Stieglitz who owned an art gallery. Stieglitz, at the time, was considered one of America's best photographers, and Georgia would become one of his main subjects for his photography. Her nude pictures would be exhibited and make her a household name in New York. Also, she became well known for her own art which contained New York City scenes and natural forms such as flowers. While in her thirties, she became a renowned American artist. In 1928, a set of her paintings sold for the highest amount ever paid for a set of paintings by a living American artist. Her husband would die and Georgia, at the age of sixty-one, would begin a new life by moving from her home in New York to Abiquiu, New Mexico, where she, for the rest of her life, would paint the scenes of that state. At seventy-one she took a break from her painting and embarked on a three and one-half month trip around the world. Her vitality and energy was such that at age seventy-four, Georgia was rafting down the Colorado River. At age seventy-seven, Ms. O'Keefe painted the largest painting of her career on a 24 x 8 foot canvas — 192 square feet. Her art continued to be admired by the public, and at age eighty-three, Georgia had an exhibition of her work at the Whitney Museum of American Art in New York City. Unfortunately, at age eighty-four, she lost her central vision from eye degeneration, but rather than giving up the arts, she started a new career in pottery since she could use her hands to feel with and not rely on her eyes as much as she had in the past. However, she was determined to paint, and at age eighty-nine, using her memory and other methods, she started painting once again. That same year she would also write a book about her art. Georgia O'Keefe would continue to paint right up until her death, when she died young at age ninety-eight.

Another that I discovered who never grew old was Konrad Adenauer, who was born to a Roman Catholic family of five children in 1876 in Cologne, Germany. Even though he was admitted to the practice of law, he became more interested in politics and served as Mayor of Cologne from 1917 to 1933. But, in 1933, he would lose his position as Mayor of Cologne to the Nazis who had come into power in Germany. He would have to flee Cologne to avoid reprisals from the Nazis and lost everything he had. Apprehended in 1934 by the Nazis and imprisoned briefly, he was later released and hid once again from the Nazis, managing to survive until the Third Reich fell. When World War II ended, Adenauer was sixty-nine years of age, well past retirement age for most. But Adenauer, rather than give in to his misfortunes and age, re-built his life, which resulted in him becoming Mayor of Cologne once again. However, he knew that Germany had to have new leadership after the war, so he became active in a political party whose mission was to rebuild Germany; as a result, he was elected Chancellor of Germany at age seventy-three and continued as Chancellor for many years thereafter. At age seventy-seven, Adenauer was named *Time* magazine's Man of the Year, and at age eighty-one, he was once again elected Chancellor of Germany. As Chancellor, at age eighty-five, Adenauer visited the United States and met with President Kennedy. At age eighty-six, he was bestowed with the highest award given to a civilian by France when he received Le'gion d' Honneur of France. He would leave his position as Chancellor of Germany, but would continue to be involved with his nation's future. At age eighty-seven, he began writing his memoirs which he continued working on until his death at age ninety-one.

The "fountain of youth" was also discovered by Katherine Anne Porter, who was born in 1890 in Indian Creek, Texas. Although she left home at sixteen and never received a high school education, she became a college professor, a successful novelist, short story writer, and journalist. After trying acting and singing in her early years, she finally settled on writing, first for newspapers and magazines, and later, she would primarily write short stories. Most of her life, she never had money and had to make her living by her wits. She would reside in Texas, New York, Mexico City, and spent several years in Europe. This attractive sexy lady was known to drink champagne at breakfast, and would marry four times. Even though she had never received a college education, at age sixty-three, Ms. Porter was teaching writing at the University of Michigan. At age seventy, she boasted that she was learning new sexual techniques with her Latin lover. At age seventy-one, Ms. Porter finished writing *Ship of Fools*, her only novel, which became a best seller and would finally make her rich. The film rights were sold, and she became richer. Even though she had found financial security, she did not retire but continued to write, and at age seventy-five was awarded the Pulitzer Prize and the National Book Award for *The Collected Stories of Katherine Anne Porter*. She also resumed her magazine career and at age eighty-two, she covered the Cape Canaveral moon shot as a journalist for *Playboy* magazine. At age eighty-six, she published the book, *The Never-Ending Wrong*. Katherine Anne Porter would die young at age ninety and be buried in the cemetery at her birthplace, Indian Creek, Texas.

Another among those I studied who never grew old and stayed young throughout his life was Leslie Townes Hope, better known as Bob Hope. Born in 1903 in Eltham, London, England, Hope's family would immigrate to the

United States and settle in Cleveland, Ohio when he was five years old. This amazing man's career would consist of acting as a comedian in vaudeville, radio, television, and movies. Writing or contributing to fifteen books, hosting the Academy Awards ceremony eighteen times, and appearing in more than fifty movies with cameo appearances in another fifteen, he would be involved in broadcasting for sixty-four years. He also made sixty tours throughout the world with the United Service Organization bringing much enjoyment to American troops abroad. Hope apparently learned how to stay young from his grandfather, whom he said was still riding his bicycle to the pub at age ninety-nine. When most people are drawing their first social security check, Bob Hope, at sixty-five, was making a Christmas tour to entertain U.S. troops stationed in the Far East. This tour would take him to Korea, Okinawa, Thailand, South Viet Nam, the Philippine Islands, and Guam where he performed thirty shows in fourteen days. Hope was a constant entertainer, which sometimes required him to travel as many as 20,000 miles per week. At age sixty-six, once again, Hope was off to the Far East to entertain the troops. The televised shows of this Far East tour resulted in the largest entertainment program in television history until that time. Even though he never finished high school, he would receive a high school diploma at age seventy-two. He treasured this diploma, but by this time, he had already received thirty-two honorary college degrees due to his selfless service to his country. Even in his 80th year, he would to continue to entertain, and that year, he completed 174 engagements as a performer, six television specials, forty-two benefits, eighty-six personal appearances, and fourteen golf tournaments. Once again, at age eighty-four, Hope was in the Persian Gulf for another Christmas show. He never slowed down. At age eighty-six, Hope performed a live act with George Burns at Madison Square Gardens.

At age eighty-seven,   he was in Saudi Arabia for a Christmas show for the U.S. troops who fought in Desert Storm. Reaching the age of ninety, when most have left this world, Hope was playing nine holes of golf at least four times a week and was booked up for six months with performances. In addition, he signed a two year contract with NBC for eight more specials. For his devotion to the Armed Services through the years, at age ninety-four, by a special act of Congress, Bob Hope became an Honorary Veteran of the Armed Forces of America. At age ninety-five, once again, he was before the public, making an appearance at the Emmy awards. He would continue entertaining and staying young until his death at age 100.

Leni, Bob Hope, and the many others convinced me that retaining youth or staying young is a way of life and that it is not just reserved for the young in age. Also, I realized that there are also many with us today whom I believe have found the "fountain of youth". For instance, as I write, when I think of "young" in today's world, I not only think of a child riding a bike for the first time, I also think of P. D. James, at eighty, penning another mystery novel. I think of the blues legend B.B. King still playing his music at eighty as he did at thirty, who, when asked when he would retire, he answered "about eight to ten years after I'm dead." And I think of Clint Eastwood, at eighty, directing another movie. I think of the crooner Tony Bennett still performing at eighty-five as he did at thirty-five, saying "I'll never retire". And the active actress Betty White, who celebrated her 90th birthday party with an NBC Special. These people are still living their lives to the fullest and are not sitting in a rocking chair on their front porches. They know that life is like a parade with time marching on, and they have chosen to be in a band or on a float, rather than being lost in the crowds watching it all pass by.

I had now found numerous people who stayed young throughout their lives, regardless of their lifestyle, who all obviously found something to keep them from growing old. They had all seemingly found the "fountain of youth", but I still wasn't sure what they all had in common that gave them this youthful outlook on life which kept them from growing old. What was it? It was not until I studied a poem that was given to me on my birthday that I would learn what they all had in common.

CHAPTER 7

GENERAL DOUGLAS MacARTHUR
AND THE POEM THAT KEPT HIM YOUNG

"Age wrinkles the body.
Quitting wrinkles the soul."
MacArthur

On my 60th birthday, I was given a hand-written poem as a gift from a very good friend. The poem was beautifully written for she had obviously spent many hours transcribing it with her calligraphy pen. I guess she thought I was getting old, for the poem is about how to stay young. It was supposedly authored by General Douglas MacArthur, and she so inscribed it accordingly. As I read the verses that day, I felt as though I had seen it before, but I did not associate it with MacArthur. This puzzled me. I wondered whether or not he was the true author. I was not at a time in my project when I would have recognized the importance of the poem, particularly since I was not aware of its history. Also, it was a busy time in my law practice and in my life in that I was still in the midst of raising and educating children, so I put it aside. A few years later, I would see an article in the newspaper that mentioned a poem named *Youth*. This piqued my interest once again, so I re-visited the question about whether or not General Douglas MacArthur was the true author of the poem, and if not, who was?

Curiosity took control, and I turned from my project to research this question, not realizing that it would probably become the most important piece of the puzzle that had plagued me over the years. It was like discovering the map which would take me to the treasure.

What I learned and discovered was that the author of the poem I had been given on my birthday was not MacArthur, but was instead, a little-known poet by the name of Samuel Ullman. The poem was written in 1918 by Ullman when he was seventy-eight years of age. Ullman lived in Birmingham, Alabama, and had retired from the business world to pursue a life-long ambition to write poetry. Of the many poems he would write, one was entitled *Youth.* The poem was published in 1922 by Ullman, but little was known of its existence at the time, and it soon faded into obscurity. Ullman would die in 1924, never knowing the impact that his poem would someday have on world events. With this information, I began to wonder: If Samuel Ullman was the true author of the poem, why was MacArthur named the author on my poem?

In 1941, General Douglas MacArthur was stationed in the Philippine Islands where he was the Military Commander. On December 7th of that year, Pearl Harbor was attacked by the Japanese. In a matter of hours, the Philippine Islands were also attacked. At the time of the attack of the Philippine Islands, MacArthur had only 22,000 U.S. soldiers and 80,000 Filipinos under his command, whereas, the Japanese had over 6 million men under arms. The attack consisted of relentless bombing over many weeks which completely destroyed the main air base, Clark Field, cutting off any means of escape by air by MacArthur and his men, nor could they receive new supplies or troops to help defend the islands. The onslaught by the Japanese would continue, and, in time, it was obvious that the Japanese would be successful in capturing the Islands. Time was running out for MacArthur and his soldiers. In fact, Tokyo Rose predicted that MacArthur would soon be captured and hung in Tokyo's Imperial Palace. Even though MacArthur was ready to die with his troops, he would be ordered by President Roosevelt to abandon his men and flee by boat to Australia. Reluctantly, on March 15, 1942, the General followed the President's order and left the Philippines and his men. It was at this point that he made his famous declaration, "I shall return."

MacArthur, his wife, and his son were transported through enemy lines and made their way to Australia. MacArthur was sixty-two years old at the time. It was a time when sixty was considered old. He had already retired once and appeared to have no real purpose or direction in his life; but he had been re-activated because of the impending threat of war. He was not in the best of health, and he had been advised by his doctors that it may be dangerous to continue active service. Stuck in Australia, he was being ridiculed back home for abandoning his troops and was being referred to as "Dugout Doug" — some claiming he hid from the relentless bombing of the Philippines by the Japanese while his troops died. He also knew that when he left the Islands for Australia, his troops would be at the mercy of the Japanese, and there would be heartless treatment suffered by his men. His fears were realized; for shortly after his departure, no longer being able to defend themselves, his men would surrender to the Japanese. Subjected to a march, known as the Bataan Death March, of sixty miles without food and very little water, his men were beheaded, starved, and beaten. Thousands died. Those who did complete the march were imprisoned and remained under harsh conditions for the duration of the war with only the hope that MacArthur would return as promised.

At the time of his arrival in Australia, MacArthur was given command of all of the Allied troops in the Pacific; however, there were no troops to command. He could only wait until troops arrived. This would take many months. All the while, the Japanese continued to usurp most of the Pacific in their relentless waging of war. Because of his age, his health, the ridicule, and the leaving of his troops, MacArthur had perhaps reached the lowest point of his life. But little did he know that he would receive a letter that contained a poem which would change his entire life.

The Americans back home knew of MacArthur's plight, and had begun to write him in Australia. Before long, he was receiving as many as one hundred and fifty letters a day. It was at this time that someone sent him a letter that contained a poem called "How to Stay Young". No author was given, but MacArthur was so taken by this poem that he had it framed and hung on his office wall. The poem was continuously read by him, and key words were memorized to the extent that they became a part of Douglas MacArthur. He would live by those words. The poem also became so associated with MacArthur that many believed it had been written by him.

MacArthur finally got his army. With the words of the poem instilled in him, he had a means for new inspiration and a fresh outlook on life. He would steadily lead his troops two thousand miles across the Pacific for the next two years. The Japanese would lose time and time again. Making eighty-seven landings, he would inspect war zones, disregarding his own safety acting as if he were a young soldier once again. Also, defying his age and perhaps drawing on his wisdom that he found from the poem, MacArthur led his troops to bring down the Japanese military and the defeat of Japan. In the process, MacArthur, on October 20, 1944, would wade onto the shores of Leyte Island of the Philippines, fulfilling his promise to return, and would thereafter, free those men whom he had left behind.

Finally, on the 2nd day of September, 1945, he would accept the surrender of Japan on the U.S.S. Missouri.

By the time of the Japanese surrender, four years of war would have taken its toll on any man, but not MacArthur. As a result of the poem, he now knew how to stay young. Even though he was sixty-five years of age at the end of the war, he would not go home, but instead, he would assume the major task of the occupation of Japan. One of the first things he did was to hang his treasured poem on his office wall in Tokyo as he had done in Australia. With the war now over, MacArthur continued to rely on his new-found youth and set to work. His mission was to rebuild and reshape a country, describing his job accordingly, "I had to be an economist, a political scientist, an engineer, a manufacturing executive, a teacher, even a theologian of sorts." He worked seven days a week, including Christmas and his birthday, never taking a vacation for the next five years and would never lose a day to illness. He permitted himself only the following diversions from his duty – reading, private movie showings, and football.

With the vitality of a thirty year old, MacArthur would reform the Japanese government by requiring women's suffrage, encouraging unionization, liberating courses in schools, ending monopolies for a wider distribution of income, and promotion of trade. He launched public health and agriculture programs, increased broadcasting coverage, and implemented new laws for civil rights, property rights, divorce, and equal rights for women. He gave the war-devastated country hope. He even wrote and gave the Japanese people a new Constitution.

MacArthur continued in his role as the leader of

occupied Japan until June 24, 1950, when South Korea was invaded by North Korea. Even though he was now seventy years of age, once again contending that he was still young, MacArthur took command of all U.N. Forces to oppose the North Koreans. In this role, he would prove once again that age doesn't necessarily have boundaries. Opposing younger military advisors, he again drew on his wisdom and did what was thought to be impossible by landing his troops at Inchon, South Korea, and not elsewhere on the Korean peninsula. Inchon had high sea walls, could be easily mined, and was considered one of the worst possible landing sites, but, MacArthur knew that the North Koreans would not suspect a landing at this location. He was right. By landing at Inchon it allowed MacArthur and his troops to surprise the North Koreans and eventually drive them back to the 38th parallel.

MacArthur wanted to continue his command of the U.N. forces and defeat the North Koreans, but a personality conflict arose between MacArthur and President Truman which resulted in MacArthur being relieved of his command. It was a set-back for him, but he did not let it affect his youthful outlook. Nevertheless, his career in the Far East was over. He then returned to the States. It would be his first time to set foot in the continental United States in fourteen years; he was now seventy-one years of age.

When he returned to the United States, it was like Caesar returning to Rome. He spoke before a joint session of Congress for thirty-four minutes and was interrupted with thirty ovations. In addition, he visited several cities throughout the United States and received a motorcade parade in New York City which was nineteen miles long — millions turned out to greet him; even 40,000 longshoremen walked off their jobs to be there. Douglas MacArthur would never retire from the military and would go on to advise presidents and Congress. He became Board Chairman of Remington Rand Corporation at the age of seventy-two. When MacArthur was seventy-five, he spoke at the Ambassador Hotel in Los Angeles stating that he was still young and using some of the words in his speech from the poem. MacArthur would return once again to the Philippines in 1961, giving a speech in Manilla which was attended by over one million people. In his eighties, he hand-wrote his memoirs of 213,000 words, finishing on the day of his 84th birthday and would die young that same year.

MacArthur wasn't the only one who profited from this poem. It seems that the entire Japanese nation would benefit from the words of the poem as well. In 1945 *Reader's Digest,* having heard of MacArthur's reverence for the poem, discovered the true author, and published it in one of their magazines. The Japanese soldiers, after surrendering and returning from the war to their homeland, would read the poem, and as Japan was re-building their country, it became known throughout the Japanese community. The poem continued to be circulated in Japan over the next several years when inspiration was so needed by the Japanese people, especially in the business community. For example, in 1965 one Japanese businessman related that he was reluctant to take on the leadership of a major business enterprise because he was seventy years old at the time. But upon learning of the poem, he realized that he could stay young and accomplish this task. He, like MacArthur, memorized parts of the poem and set to work. He was so enthralled by the words of the poem and how it had affected him, that he sent twenty thousand copies to other businessmen throughout the world. At age ninety-two this gentleman would reminiscence about how he found a renewed vigor from the words of the poem. Even in 1985 it was so revered that an organization was formed in Japan called "The Youth Association". Its objectives were to study the poem and other works of similar value. The Association grew into 150 corporate members and 1,800 individual members. The Association held a celebration in 1987 honoring the poem and Ullman. At this time one of the attendees said that the poem was to the Japanese people what spinach was to Popeye — a source of vitality. It is clear that the poem played a major role in the rebuilding of Japan by sustaining the Japanese mind with its inspiring message. Here is Samuel Ullman's poem that so affected MacArthur and the people of Japan:

Youth

Youth is not a time of life; it is a state of mind;
it is not a matter of rosy cheeks,
red lips and supple knees;
it is a matter of the will, a quality of the imagination,
a vigor of the emotions;
it is the freshness of the deep springs of life.

Youth means a temperamental predominance
of courage
over timidity of the appetite,
for adventure over the love of ease.
This often exists in a man of sixty
more than a boy of twenty.

Nobody grows old merely by a number of years.
We grow old by deserting our ideals.
Years may wrinkle the skin,
but to give up enthusiasm wrinkles the soul.
Worry, fear, self-distrust bows the heart
and turns the spirit back to dust.

Whether sixty or sixteen,
there is in every human being's heart
the lure of wonder,
the unfailing child-like appetite of what's next,
and the joy of the game of living.

In the center of your heart and my heart
there is a wireless station;
so long as it receives messages of beauty,
hope, cheer, courage and power
from men and from the Infinite,
so long are you young.

When the aerials are down,
and your spirit is covered with snows of cynicism
and the ice of pessimism,
then you are grown old,
even at twenty,
but as long as your aerials are up,
to catch the waves of optimism,
there is hope you may die young at eighty.

CHAPTER 8

THE PURSUIT OF HAPPINESS
FINDING ENJOYMENT IN LIFE

"Happiness or misery is in one's soul."
Democritus

I had now reached another turning point in my quest. It was the poem *Youth* that revealed to me the main ingredient which kept all of the people young whom I had studied. That is, they all kept "their aerials up" throughout their lives. Now I wanted to hone in on those individual subjects that were alluded to in Ullman's poem. So I broke down the poem and divided it into the messages that Ullman is giving us through his poem which I believe are important to maintain youth, and then I resumed my research. The first subject that I delved into was happiness. Even though the word "happiness" does not appear in Ullman's poem, I believe it is clear that he was speaking of happiness when he wrote words such as "joy in the game of living".

Napoleon once said that all a man needs for happiness is food and clothing, a hut, a wife, allow him to work, eat, beget, and sleep and he will be happier than a prince. I found it takes very little to be happy, but I don't believe that achieving happiness is quite as simple as Napoleon said. Happiness has always been one of the main objectives of human life and has been a major discussion by philosophers throughout the ages. I probably encountered more quotes on happiness than any other subject, and a recent study indicates that there may even be a relationship between happiness and longevity.

Happiness can be defined as good fortune, pleasure, contentment, blessedness, enjoyment, satisfaction, and I'm sure others. Probably for every person there is a different description of what happiness is. Some say acquiring wealth will bring happiness; others say it's found in good health; and yet others say it's found in our work. Regardless of the definition that is given, I've found that you must be in love with life. Being in love with life is being in love with all things which life has to offer; thus, to find happiness, you must maintain this frame of mind.

One of the happiest people I studied was Helen Keller, even though she was blind and deaf. She could not see the sky above, nor the scenery on the earth; she could not see the flowers in the morning, the moon at night, nor could she hear the birds sing or beautiful music play, yet she considered her life happy. Explaining her happiness, she said, "My life has been happy because I have had wonderful friends and plenty of interesting work to do. I seldom think about my limitations, and they never make me sad. Perhaps there is just a touch of yearning at times, but it is vague, like a breeze among flowers. The wind passes and the flowers are content." Ms. Keller went on to say, "So I try to make the light in others' eyes my sun, the music in others' ears my symphony, the smile on others' lips my happiness... Everything has its wonders, even darkness and silence, and I learn, whatever state I may be in, therein to be content." Even though she lived in dark silence, she made it part of her life to spread her happiness all over the world throughout her long life. She is proof of the Roman Emperor Marcus Aurelius' maxim, "Very little is needed to make a happy life" because Helen Keller loved life.

Also, the Japanese philosopher, Kaibara Ekken, agrees with Marcus Aurelius when he tells us that happiness can easily be found in the world around us. Ekken went on to say that, "Those who can enjoy the beauty in the Heaven above and the Earth beneath need not envy the luxury of the rich...The scenery is constantly changing. No two mornings or two evenings are quite alike... Loving flowers, I rise early; Loving the moon, I retire late...."

Also, there appears to be no excuse for not finding happiness. Epictetus, the ancient Roman sage, said, "If a man is unhappy, this must be his own fault; for God made all men to be happy." In fact, happiness can be found in almost any circumstance. When I read the journal during the first voyage around the world of Captain Cook, it became clear to me that happiness is not found through wealth, possessions, or the like. But like staying young, it must be found within oneself. When Captain Cook would see the natives of New Holland (now Australia) for the first time, he would write in his journal that they appeared to be the most "wretched people on earth; but in reality, they are far more happier than we Europeans, being wholly unacquainted, not only with the superfluous, but with the necessary conveniences so much sought after in Europe; they're happy in not knowing the use of them. They live in a tranquility which is not disturbed by the inequality of condition. The earth and sea of their own accord furnishes them with all things necessary for life. They covet not magnificent houses, household - stuff, etc.; they live in a warm and fine climate, and enjoy every wholesome air, so they have very little need of clothing; and this they seem to be fully sensible of, for many to whom we gave cloth, etc., left it carelessly upon the sea beach and in the woods, as a thing they had no manner of use for; in short, they seemed to set no value upon anything we gave them, nor would they ever part with anything of their own for any one article we could offer."

In addition to loving life, to find happiness, I found that one also needs to stay connected with others. Not only will it help bring happiness, I've learned it is essential to staying young. The Austrian psychotherapist, Dr. Alfred Adler, said that individuals who are not interested in their fellow men have the "greatest difficulties in life." In fact, he said it is from such individuals "that all failures spring." According to Dr. Charles Eliot, former President of Harvard University, in his book *The Happy Life,* "The most satisfactory thing in all this earthly life is to be able to serve our fellow beings, first those who are bound to us by ties of love, then the wider circle of fellow townsmen, fellow-countrymen or fellow-men." Also, centenarian A. Prentiss Fatheree, of Jackson, Mississippi once stated, "In my long life I have observed that true happiness is achieved by what we do for others and not what is done for us." In fact, the noted writer, C. S. Lewis, felt so strongly about being connected with others that he warned of the consequences of not engaging with our fellow men, which may bring about misery, rather than happiness. He said, "If you want to make sure of keeping it intact, you must give your heart to no one, not even to an animal. Wrap it carefully round with hobbies and little luxuries. Avoid all entanglements; lock it up safe in the casket or coffin of your selfishness. But in that casket - safe, dark, motionless, airless – it will change. It will not be broken; it will become unbreakable, impenetrable, irredeemable." Also, like Lewis, Dr. Samuel Johnson, the old English sage, warns us that, "If a man does not make new acquaintances as he advances through life, he will soon find himself left alone. A man, Sir, should keep his friendship in constant repair."

Thus, it is obvious that one of the elements of

happiness is interaction with other people. Even the ancient philosopher, Aristotle, brings this to our attention: "It is, I think, absurd to place the happy man in solitude, as no one would choose to possess the whole world by himself, for man is a social being and disposed to live with others. It follows that a happy man must live in society, for he possesses all that is by nature good." Booker T. Washington once said, "I have found that the happiest people are those who do the most for others; the most miserable are those who do the least." On the lighter side, Dale Messick, the creator of the Brenda Starr comic strip, truly enjoyed staying connected. She was so connected in her eighties that she claimed she had three boyfriends at the same time, but stated, "All three wouldn't make one good man, but at my age, you can't be too choosy."

As I moved along, one of the questions I asked myself — can we pursue happiness? When Thomas Jefferson wrote the *Declaration of Independence,* it appeared that he thought happiness was so important in our lives that he made it an integral part of the *Declaration of Independence* when he wrote the words that men are endowed with the unalienable right of "the pursuit of Happiness". Those words of Jefferson seem to imply that to find happiness, it must be pursued. But I believe Jefferson got it wrong. I have learned that we don't find our happiness by pursuing it, but, instead, we find it by pursuing other things besides happiness, and through the pursuit of those other things, that is where we find our happiness. It is the absorption in other things besides ourselves where the roots of happiness grow. Nathaniel Hawthorne said it this way: "Happiness in this world, when it comes, comes incidentally. Make it the object of pursuit and it leads us on a wild goose chase, and is never attained. Follow some other object, and very possibly we

may find we have caught happiness without dreaming of it."
In fact, this applied to Jefferson himself, for he found
happiness, but it was in his emersion of his many activities
as he grew older, and not in a pursuit of happiness in itself.
In his own words, he advocated that "our own happiness
requires that we should continue to mix with the world, and
to keep pace with it." He did this in a big way. After he left
the presidency, his days were full; his activities were many;
his beloved home, Monticello, and its grounds were a
constant beehive; he corresponded with people all over the
world; he read constantly; and never stopped learning.
Furthermore, he designed and physically laid out the
University of Virginia campus and oversaw the construction
of the buildings and grounds. Jefferson continued these
pursuits throughout his long life and remained happy. He
had a reason to get up in the morning; he had a "to do" list
and worked diligently each day to pursue his many tasks
that he had designed for himself. Though he had all of the
problems that accompany aging, he always looked at every
aspect of life in a positive manner, losing himself in
something other than himself. Thus, long-lasting and
purposeful happiness is found in the pursuit of worthwhile
endeavors that make you forget about yourself. It's like the
old paradox: "To find your life, you must first lose it."

Where we go wrong is in the things that we pursue
in trying to find happiness. Any wrongful pursuit can cause
one to fall into one of the seven deadly sins — pride, wrath,
envy, lust, gluttony, sloth, and avarice. These pursuits only
deal with oneself, and not others. For instance, if we pursue
wealth we may find happiness in the original pursuit, but if
we become consumed by the pursuit, then it can turn into
avarice. Even frugality, if sought to excess, can become a
form of avarice.

It has been said that avarice is a major vice of the declining years, and one that all of us must be aware of and not allow ourselves to fall into this trap. Therefore, I spent some quality time on this topic, since it obviously can destroy happiness and obstruct our ability to stay young. Avarice means greed, selfishness, stinginess, hoarding, and being miserly. The philosopher, Zeno, tells us, "The avaricious man is like the barren sandy ground of the desert which sucks in all the rain and dews with greediness, but yields no fruitful herbs or plants for the benefit of others."

I even encountered a man in my law practice who had succumbed to avarice to such an extent that he complained of the amount of toilet tissue being used by his family. But one of the worst cases of avarice that I encountered was several years ago when I was called on to give advice to an eighty-three year old man who had scrimped and saved his entire life. He lived on a small farm in a simple home with very few modern conveniences. He had denied his wife any modern appliances, only allowing her to have the bare essentials of clothing and things needed for daily life. Except for the necessities of life, all income produced was to be saved – not spent. He had little education, had no particular skills or crafts, working at only common-labor jobs. But even through these means, he had saved a small fortune. However, because of his age and his failing health, he was faced with the possibility of a nursing home or death. Either scenario, he worried that the government might take his money through taxes or otherwise that he had saved all of his life. Tears were rolling down his cheeks as he explained his quandary. This man had never truly lived, for he had succumbed to avarice in the worst way. He had chased a false dream.

An example of how ridiculous avarice can be is described in one of *Aesop's Fables.* The fable tells us of a miser who treasured a lump of gold which he kept buried in a hole in the ground, and went to look at his treasure each daily. Unfortunately, his hiding place was discovered by another, and the lump of gold was stolen. The miser was overcome with grief as a result of his loss, but it was pointed out to him that the only thing he ever did was look at it each day, rather than utilizing it for himself or others. So it might as well have been a plain stone since he did not make the slightest use of the gold anyway. The miser, like my two examples, was living for the wrong reasons.

Avarice is a selfish pursuit. I once read that "happiness begins when selfishness ends" and "materialism is toxic for happiness." According to Seneca, "If what you have seems insufficient to you, then though you possess the world, you will yet be miserable." Benjamin Franklin said it this way: "Avarice and happiness never saw each other." Bertrand Russell, who faced every aspect of life, both ups and downs, knew what was important in order to avoid avarice. He said, "It is the preoccupation with possessions, more than anything else that prevents men from living freely and nobly." Hulda Crooks, who certainly found happiness, particularly in her latter years, lived in a small studio apartment, for she said that anything bigger would just require having more "junk". Hufeland said, "Avarice consumes itself." *The Book of Common Prayer* reminds us, "We brought nothing into this world, and it is certain we can carry nothing out."

But leaving the negatives and getting back to the positives, I've learned that if you want to be happy, you need to enjoy yourself. When I think of enjoying yourself, I recall a popular song from my childhood by the bandleader, Guy Lombardo, entitled "Enjoy Yourself". It was a lively tune and had a message that all of us need to heed. The stanzas sung by Kenny Gardner and The Lombardo Trio made it clear that you need to enjoy yourself for it is later than you think. Along these same lines, a friend of mine who always appears to be happy said that once he figured out that he was not going to get out of this world alive, he decided to enjoy himself. Today, he is in his eighties and still enjoying himself.

But how can we enjoy ourselves? One way is to seek out small pleasures that are available to us everyday. According to Benjamin Franklin, "happiness consists more in small conveniences of pleasure that occur every day..." And from what I learned about Franklin, he knew a lot about this. Pleasures can come from many sources. One is from music. Plato said, "Through music the soul learns harmony and rhythm." In fact, in the 19th century, the German philosopher, Friedrich Nietzsche, felt so strongly that we need music in our lives that he said, "Without music, life would be a mistake." Also, in my studies of history, I was surprised to learn that music was a main entertainment for the Greeks, and that musicians flourished in Greece. The Egyptians were so involved with music that they actually had bands which could be composed of harps, pipes, flutes, guitars, lyres, and tambourines. At one festival of the Egyptians, more than six hundred musicians were employed. Music has always been a way to achieve some small pleasure of happiness throughout civilization.

In addition, another small pleasure or enjoyment which can bring about happiness may be found through art. How wonderful it is to have an uplifting feeling when we see beautiful artwork. We can adorn our houses with it, we can seek it in museums, and we can see it in nature. And not only can one experience art in this manner, you might can produce it yourself. For instance, painting was one of the ways that Churchill enjoyed himself and found happiness. It constituted his relaxation and pastime. He even claimed that he enjoyed it so much that he couldn't live without painting.

Still some of us may find our small pleasures or enjoyment - thus happiness - in travel. If you have money, there are luxury cruises that can take you all over the world to see the many sights and countries this earth has to offer. But if the money is not there, there are still many sights that can be seen without major airline trips or tour costs. Every state in America has its own natural wonders and attractions that are not expensive to enjoy. Travel does not necessarily have to mean spending a lot of money. For example, a very adventuresome Ned and Mary Walker, at ages sixty-nine and sixty-seven, respectively, rode their Harley Davidson motorcycle from their home in Mississippi to Alaska in 2008 covering 11,000 miles which included seventeen states and Canada.

Sporting activities may also give many people enjoyment and bits of happiness, whether as a spectator or as an active participant in the game. John D. Rockefeller, Sr. (who did not take up golf until age sixty) said that the game brought him happiness and even claimed that it lengthened his life and improved his health. Of course, your television is full of many channels which can bring you football and basketball games, racing, and just about every other form of sport you may want to watch from your armchair.

Others may find some of these simple pleasures of happiness in gardening, whether vegetables or flowers, or in the overall landscaping of one's yard. Konrad Adenauer found his enjoyment in his garden — there is something to be said for digging in the dirt, watching things grow, having cut flowers each day to add to the ambiance of your home, or eating a plate of fresh vegetables for dinner.

To find these little bits of happiness that Franklin spoke of, there are probably hundreds of hobbies available to us, and I'm sure there is at least one we can find to enjoy. And remember, one of the best ways to express happiness is through laughter. A good hearty laugh is good for the soul, one's health, and I've even read that laughing may lengthen your life.

Also if you want to enjoy yourself, there are times in your life that you need to let go of the restrictions that have been placed on you — whether by yourself or others. You can be a "peach" or you can be a "prune". "Peaches" have more fun and are happier. The pianist, Arthur Rubinstein, said, "Happiness is to live. It is the only happiness possible." He declared, "What good are vitamins? Eat a lobster, eat a pound of caviar — live!" Rubinstein would live fully and die young at age ninety-five.

Along these lines, I'll never forget an incident when my wife and I had dinner at a restaurant in our hometown. The restaurant was known for its excellent spicy food. The restaurant was in an old bank, with its fixtures intact; depending on your seating arrangement, you may be in the old vault, the bank officer's area, or in the tellers' cages. We were seated in the teller cages along with an elderly couple who were passing through town while on vacation. We were so close it was impossible not to overhear what was said at each other's tables. The couple shared a little of their story with us while we waited for our food. They had heard that the restaurant served the best food in town, and they were visiting our town to soak in the atmosphere and to eat delicious food. However, when the waitress took their order, she was instructed that their food was not to contain any salt, pepper, or other seasonings, and particular instructions were given for the preparation of their food because he was on a strict diet. All I could think of listening to this litany, was why were they here? How can the food be good if not prepared according to the chef's instructions? Why were they on vacation if they weren't going to enjoy themselves? Before long, I realized that I was sitting next to a couple of "prunes". I don't believe that Arthur Rubinstein would have approved of this couple's means of enjoying themselves. Also, when it comes to "prunes", I once read that people who are always taking care of their health are like misers, who are hoarding up a treasure which they will never have the spirit to enjoy.

As for "prunes", John D. Rockefeller could be put at the top of the list. At his meals, Rockefeller would eat a plain diet of peas, beans, rice, fish, brown bread, and potatoes. He would never overeat; never eat hot food; and waited for his dishes to cool, believing that food was only to maintain life and not to be enjoyed. Chewing his food at least ten times, he also stayed at the table after eating until he considered his food was properly digested.

There's nothing new about enjoying yourself in this life. In fact, the Sumerian epic of *Gilgamesh,* considered one of the oldest known works in literature written thousands of years ago on twelve clay tablets, told us how we should live and thus find happiness:

FROM THE EPIC OF GILGAMESH

"O Gilgamesh, why dost thou run in all directions?
The life that thou seekest thou wilt not find.
When the Gods created mankind
they determined death for mankind;
Life they kept in their own hands.
Thou, O Gilgamesh, fill thy belly;
Day and night be thou merry;...
Day and night be joyous and content!
Let thy garments be pure,
Thy head be washed; wash thyself with water!
Regard the little one who takes hold of thy hand;
Enjoy the wife in thy bosom."

CHAPTER 9

PURPOSE AND DIRECTION

"Purpose is what gives life a meaning."
                                    Charles H. Parkhurst

General Douglas MacArthur, before the attack on the Philippines, was floundering, possibly dwelling on his health, his age, and appeared to have no real mission in his life. Perhaps he was on the verge of "deserting" his "ideals". It would take a war with Japan to remind him that he was a soldier, and that his purpose was to defeat the Japanese; he would carry out this mission. For the rest of his life, he would always have a central purpose. The British philosopher, James Allen, said that without a central purpose, we will become "easy prey to petty worries, fears, troubles, and self-pitying... all of which lead to ... failure, unhappiness, and loss...." Allen further stated that, "A man should conceive of a legitimate purpose in his heart, and set out to accomplish it." He tells us that a person should make this purpose the "centralizing point of his thoughts." Thus, in order to stay young, one must have a purpose. In other words, a reason for living, a mission in your life; if not, then, as Ullman pointed out, "we grow old by deserting our ideals."

When I think of purpose, the person who immediately comes to my mind is the 18th century Anglican minister, John Wesley, who founded the Methodist movement throughout England and Scotland, which spread to North America. At age eighty-six, Wesley wrote the following entry in his journal on New Year's Day, 1790: "I am now an old man, decayed from head to foot. My eyes

118

are dim, my right hand shakes much, my mouth is hot and dry every morning, I have a lingering fever almost every day... However, blessed be God, I do not slack my labor. I can preach and write still." Even under these conditions, he continued preaching and performing his duties as head of the Methodist movement throughout England and Scotland. During his lifetime, Wesley would preach more than 40,000 sermons, travel over 250,000 miles, mainly walking or riding a horse. Regardless of the weather, Wesley preached to the common man on street corners and any other places that were available for the public to hear his word. His evangelical preaching was frowned upon by the Church of England which caused him to be slandered, stoned, man-handled, and ridiculed, but, regardless, Wesley kept preaching anyway until his death at eighty-seven, for it was his chosen purpose. His persistence paid off. Wesley was eventually revered and honored, and today there are over 33 million Methodists.

In more recent times, James Michener, the author of such books as *Texas* and *Hawaii*, at age seventy-nine, faced a crucial point in his life. His health was deteriorating; he was suffering from attacks of vertigo; and he had to have by-pass heart surgery, a hip replacement, and major dental work. With these health issues and being well past normal retirement age, he was faced with a major decision regarding what he should do with the rest of his life. He could well afford retirement, for he was rich from his many books. But he also liked writing and had other books in his mind. So what was he to do? It was at this time that he recalled when he was a young boy, a farmer who lived down the road from his home had an old apple tree that had reached a similar position in its life as had Michener. The tree was waning and failing to produce apples as it always had in the past. But the farmer did not just sit idly by while the apple tree withered away into retirement. Instead, during the spring, he drove eight rusty nails into the tree's trunk. When fall arrived, the tree produced a bumper crop of apples. The farmer told Michener that his hammering the nails into the tree was to remind it that its purpose was to produce apples. Apparently, the message was received.

Michener equated his station in life with the apple tree and realized that his purpose was to write books, and that the various physical problems and medical procedures that he had were akin to the nails driven into the trunk of the tree. Thus, he would not give in, and instead drew new energy from this experience and remembrance. In fact, he would be more prolific than ever before. Over the next five years, Michener would write eleven books, and he would never grow old, writing up until his death at age ninety.

Like Michener, the French writer and philosopher Voltaire had a central purpose in this life through his writings at a time when France and other parts of Europe were ruled by kings and queens and man was subjected to the edicts of the Roman Catholic Church. Voltaire fought for freedom of religion, the right to a fair trial, freedom of speech, and freedom of the press. Through his writings, he proved that the pen could be mightier than the sword. It was a time that if one wrote or spoke against the establishment they could be jailed and even executed. For his positions and views, Voltaire would spend time in prison, and for most of his life, in exile from France; but much of the freedom finally won by the people of France would result from his works. Voltaire, with a youthful outlook on life, pursued his purpose until his death at the age of eighty-three, writing fifteen million words in his lifetime.

A central purpose can even give one a reason to

live, and much can be achieved, not only for one's own self, but for others. Another remarkable example of how one can achieve much through his purpose in life was Mahatma Gandhi. Gandhi, who had been a successful lawyer in South Africa where he had lived most of his life, made a conscious and determined decision to return to his home country, India, and free India from the shackles of the British Empire, devoting the remainder of his life to his chosen purpose. To accomplish his mission, he would give away all of his possessions to the poor, except for three sets of clothing — two for his daily wear and one to sleep in. For the rest of his life, he slept on a bare earthen floor and usually travelled by foot. His food would only consist of nuts, lemons, oranges, dates, rice, and goat's milk. He would take no medicine and used fasting for many purposes. Gandhi would lead the people of India, using nonviolent demonstrations and other means of civil disobedience. When imprisoned for his actions, he would fast until the British freed him in fear that he would become a martyr if he died in a British cell. Through these unconventional means, Gandhi accomplished his purpose on August 15, 1947, when India achieved independence, ending one hundred and ninety years of British rule. Unfortunately, at age seventy-nine, on January 30, 1948, Gandhi died of an assassin's bullet. But prior to his death, Gandhi's feat had been accomplished without violence or major conflicts. Gandhi attained the object of his purpose as a private citizen without wealth, never holding an official title or post. Yet he became, as U.S. General George Marshall said, "... the spokesman for the conscience of all mankind."

Picasso found his life's purpose in art. He was a ceramist, lithographer, sculptor, draftsman, and of course, one of the world's most renowned painters. His works would sell for millions. In his eighty-seventh year, Picasso produced one hundred sixty-five paintings and forty-five drawings, which were exhibited at the Palace of Popes in Avignon, France. He pursued his mission relentlessly until his death at the age of ninety-one. Another who found his purpose in art was Renoir, who in his seventies was still painting, even though his fingers were so gnarled and curved by arthritis that he had to clamp the paintbrush between his thumb and fist. But, he still continued to paint, even at this age under these conditions, for it was his purpose. He declared, "I am just learning how to paint."

Throughout history people have found many ways to carry out their purpose. There stands a monument outside Wadesmill, England, with the following inscription: "On this spot where stands this monument in the month of June 1785 Thomas Clarkson resolved to devote his life to bringing about the abolition of the slave trade." Clarkson would work tirelessly throughout his life to pursue his goal by writing essays, petitioning Parliament, forming societies, and giving speeches to end what he believed was the most egregious treatment of human beings in the history of the world. Clarkson would realize his objective when in 1833 slavery was abolished throughout the British empire. The famous poet Coleridge said of Clarkson, "He ... listened to his conscience and obeyed its voice."

One of the most amazing figures I encountered who found a definite purpose for her life was a woman by the name of Mother Jones. Born in 1830, Mother Jones would die a hundred years later. She married early in life, but lost her husband and her four children in the yellow fever epidemic in Memphis, Tennessee, causing her to leave Memphis to start a new life in Chicago, Illinois, where she then lost everything she owned in the Great Chicago Fire of 1871. After these grievous misfortunes, she searched for a purpose for her life and found it by becoming a labor organizer, heading up labor movements among the mine workers in the United States. Involved in every aspect of the mine workers' lives, including child labor used in the mines, the conditions of the mines and the workers themselves, Mother Jones, in pursuing her purpose, was no push-over; she became a true fighter. At seventy-three with a head of gray and the clothes of a poor widow, she would defy government officials by speaking for the betterment of the miners and declaring, "I have been in jail more than once, and I expect to go again." In her direct manner, she stood against authority at all times. "When I know I am right fighting for those children of mine, there is no governor, no court, no president, will terrify or muzzle me." As she aged, she never lost her determination to help the miners. "I am 80 years old and I haven't long to live anyhow. Since I have to die, I would rather die for the cause to which I have given so much of my life." She was one tough cookie, but by all accounts, she was satisfied with her life, having found a purpose for her life.

Among others who found purpose in their lives was the physician Albert Schweitzer. Schweitzer made it his life's purpose in the early 20th century to found a medical and missionary hospital at Lambarene, Gabon in Africa. He is still vivid in my own memory from the news reels which showed an eighty year old with long gray hair and bushy mustache playing the organ at his African home as if he were thirty years old. He would continue his missionary work, devoting his life to the natives of Africa until his death at age ninety.

The United States Senator Claude Pepper found his purpose as a champion for the elderly by devoting most of his senatorial career by defending Social Security and Medicare and abolishing age discrimination.

Also, the famous guitarist, Andres Segovia, made it his purpose to win the same respect for the guitar as had been given to the piano, the violin, and other concert instruments. Continuing to work incessantly throughout his life to improve his art as a guitarist and pursue his goal to find the guitar's place in history, Segovia maintained a full performance schedule well into his nineties, stating, "I will have eternity to rest." Another guitarist, Jose Candido Morales (a student of the classical guitarist, Agustin Barrios) at eighty-nine years of age, suffering with cataracts, hearing problems, pain from a back injury, and arthritis, was working diligently on the mission he had given himself to record all guitar techniques that Barrios had taught so as to preserve them for future generations.

Every person can have a purpose. I have learned that each one of us needs to find that purpose. Dorothea Dix found hers. As a young schoolteacher, at age thirty-three, she suffered a complete breakdown in her health. She was told by her doctors not to work any longer at her profession and that she should not take on any strenuous activities for the rest of her life. Even though her health was in shambles, she drew on her belief that "Life is not to be expended in vain regrets." Casting aside her health problems and the warnings of her doctors, she would change her purpose from being a schoolteacher to helping those whom she believed were being mistreated in the world — the mentally ill. Dorothea Dix would spend most of the rest of her life carrying out that mission which took her throughout the United States whereby she fought for a more humane treatment of the insane by lobbying politicians for reform and speaking before legislatures which resulted in creating state institutions throughout the country for the insane. In 1845, she would write, "I have traveled ten thousand miles in three years, have visited eighteen state penitentiaries, three hundred county jails and houses of correction, more than five hundred alms houses, and other institutions. I have been happy as to promote and secure the establishment of six hospitals for the insane, several county poorhouses and several jails on a reformed plan." Her work continued until she was eighty-two when she became ill. Having no home, she was taken to the first institution which she had founded (now known as the New Jersey State Hospital) where she was cared for as a revered guest until her death. The modern treatment today for the insane is a direct result of the efforts and purpose of Dorthea Dix.

Others who found their purpose were the famous Nazi hunter, Simon Wiesenthal, who, until his retirement at age ninety-four, made it his life's purpose to bring to justice Nazi criminals, which resulted in 1,100 Nazi criminals being identified or captured. And Itche Goldberg, the Jewish writer, who died in 2006, made it his life's purpose to preserve and to pass on the Yiddish language to future generations, published his collection of essays in Yiddish on his 100th birthday.

Also, the play-write, George Bernard Shaw, set the purpose of his life towards being a dramatist. He wrote more than sixty plays, including his most famous play "Pygmalion" which was adapted into the Broadway musical "My Fair Lady". He would continue to write up until his death at ninety-four. He would say, "As long as I live I must write. If I stopped writing I should die for want of something to do." When he spoke of purpose, Shaw said that, "This is the true joy of life, the being used for a purpose recognized by yourself as a mighty one; the being thoroughly worn out before you are thrown on the scrap heap; the being a force of nature instead of a feverish selfish little clod of ailments and grievances, complaining that the world will not devote itself to making you happy."

And then there was Leo Tolstoy, who lived from 1829 to 1910, one of history's most celebrated writers whose books include *War and Peace* and *Anna Karenina*. Although he became rich from his writings, he made it his purpose in life to help the poor in Russia. Regardless of his wealth, he shunned it and lived as if he were poor so he could understand the peasantry and help them. His writings and actions influenced Gandhi and Martin Luther King, Jr. Tolstoy said, "one needs to have an aim in life."

Purpose doesn't have to be as dangerous and grandiose as Gandhi pursued. Purpose can be found by volunteering to help others; it can be your job or profession; it can be your favorite hobby, such as gardening; or it can be found in study and learning.

I found purpose can accomplish things that not only benefit mankind, but purpose can also benefit yourself. It will keep you focused on something other than yourself so you won't worry or fret about yourself. If you are a painter, like Picasso, you are concerned about the colors, the brushes, and the subject, not yourself. If you garden, like Adenauer, then you get to watch nature at its best by seeing the beautiful flowers or harvesting the fruit, not concentrating on yourself. If you volunteer, like Bob Hope, then you are concerned with others, and not yourself. If your purpose is your job or profession, then you will earn respect as well as money, and not worry about yourself. If your purpose is the study of philosophy, then you will learn

126

about history and peek at the meaning of life, but, once again, you will not be worrying about yourself. Any purpose that you choose will allow you to be absorbed in something greater than yourself, and it will give you a meaningful life. "From my earliest years," the muckraker Ida Tarbell said, "I had been told what was necessary to everyone – a purpose."

As Ida Tarbell said, having a purpose is necessary. No matter how old we are, we must have purpose in our lives if we want to stay young and not grow old. But to carry out that purpose, we must have direction. Just having a purpose will not necessarily accomplish your mission. If you have purpose without direction, it is like a ship with no rudder — you will drift upon the sea. The people I studied who stayed young had a purpose and had direction in their lives; they didn't just wake up in the morning and say, "What am I going to do today?"

A purpose will give you that reason to get up in the morning, but direction is the course, as James Allen pointed out, that you must "set out to accomplish" that purpose. You must chart a course. When I was a Boy Scout, I had a little training in the use of a compass; however, it was not until I was invited on a coon hunt did I see how a compass truly works. It would be the only coon hunt of my life. It was many years ago, but some of the hunt is still fresh in my mind. The purpose of the hunt was not to necessarily kill a raccoon, but to let the dogs run and enjoy the outing and allow the hunters to have an outing as well. Our host was the owner of about 500 acres of land, much of which was in woods. Coon hunting in Mississippi is a winter night-time sport. It is highly regarded in the South. In fact, a good coon dog, which is usually a Walker Treeing Hound, can cost over $1,000.00. This particular night, cold and damp, was fairly dark since there was a cloud cover that hid the moon. The dogs were turned out, and we entered the woods by going through a slack spot in a barbed-wire fence. The objective of the dogs was to find a raccoon. Our objective was to follow the barking dogs. Fortunately for the raccoons that night, none were found, but what amazed me about this experience was how we navigated through the woods. There were several flashlights among us, but regardless, in the woods at night all trees look the same, and there was nothing that I could see to help navigate us to and fro, particularly back home again when it was time to quit the hunt. I feared we may get lost in the dark and dreary night. Yet our host appeared to have no concerns for this fear of mine. Periodically, he would pull out his compass, shine his flashlight on it, get his bearings, and off we went in the direction along the course he set. When it was time to go home, he used the compass more frequently setting our direction along the way. In almost total darkness, with the exception of his flashlight shining on his compass, we arrived at the exact point in that barbed-wire fence from which we had departed. It was apparent at all times that our host knew exactly where he was going, even though I was lost. It is clear to me that choosing a purpose for one's life is necessary, but you must be like my coon-hunting host and know where you are going and how to get there to accomplish your purpose.

For instance, without direction, John Wesley could never have accomplished his purpose which resulted in creating the Methodist movement. He had to have a daily plan and follow through with his plans of preaching to the public, even in inclement weather. And like Wesley, Gandhi knew that to accomplish his purpose, he had to leave South Africa, give up his career, his livelihood and his possessions, and work incessantly carrying out his mission.

These men set a direction and carried it out. Thus, to accomplish your purpose, it requires direction, determination, staying focused, setting goals, allotting time, using to-do lists, and probably working with others. Who knows? Through your chosen purpose, you may also change the world. But most importantly, what I've learned is that if you want to stay young, you must have a purpose in your life. And if you want to accomplish that purpose, you must have direction.

CHAPTER 10

LEARNING AND CURIOSITY

"The longer I live, the more I read,
the more patiently I think,
the more anxiously I inquire."
John Adams

"There is so much to learn," declared Supreme Court Justice Oliver Wendell Holmes, Jr. Justice Holmes spoke those words when he was in his nineties. I've learned that no one should ever consider themselves too old to learn something knew. The people I studied who maintained their youth throughout their lives never stopped learning, and certainly, Justice Holmes was one of those people. Regardless of his age, Justice Holmes continued to learn by reading himself or by having his secretary read aloud to him by the hour, which resulted in more than four million words that they read together. When asked by President Franklin Roosevelt why he was reading Plato at his advanced age, Holmes replied, "to improve my mind."

Like Holmes, William Gladstone, the Prime Minister of England in the 19th century, never stopped learning. In addition to his own language of English, he studied Greek and Latin and read the Bible every day, often in the Greek text. Gladstone was even learning the Norwegian language at the age of seventy-five. He kept his mind sharp as a voracious reader, and during his life he would read almost 20,000 works. He kept his body sharp as well, for at age eighty-five, upon bequeathing his personal library to the St. Deiniol's Library, Gladstone, with thinning, gray hair and piercing eyes, in order to carry out his bequest, carted all

32,000 books by wheelbarrow to the library, which was a quarter of a mile away from his home. Gladstone served four times as Prime Minister during his eighty-eight years of life and was buried in Westminister Abbey with "Old Tom Parr".

Also among ancient writings we are told that Solon, the Greek statesman, continued to learn something new every day until his death at age eighty, at a time when life expectancy was less than forty. He said, "I grow old while always learning." And also among the ancients, the Greek philosopher Democritus said of learning, "I would rather discover a single demonstration (in geometry) than win the throne of Persia."

Learning appears to always have played an important role for man throughout history. It has been said that man differs only from beasts as a result of education. Without learning, man may never have developed the wheel, ink, the printing press, glass, the alphabet, paper, telephone, radio, television, computer, lightbulb, and all the other things that have helped make up the civilized world. A fact in point was found on an early papyrus writing from thousands of years ago discovered among the ruins of Egypt which contained the following quotation, "Give thy heart to learning, and love her like a mother, for there is nothing so precious as learning."

There are many ways to learn and acquire knowledge — formal or informal. Formal learning can be by attending classes such as enrolling in college courses or taking courses online. Also, there are enrichment courses that many colleges offer, including painting, languages, photography, pottery, sculpture, drawing, flower arranging, musical instruments, writing, quilting, calligraphy, landscape, interior design, geneology, journalism, music, poetry, computer courses, and many others.

There is also the opportunity to learn and travel through The Elder Hostel program. As an elder, you can become a "Road Scholar". This program was founded in 1975 for the elderly, educators, leaders, and other individuals who treasure life-long learning. It is a network of more than 1,900 colleges, universities, and independent schools, and other institutions in over seventy countries. It offers lowcost, short-term residential academic programs for adults fifty-five years of age and older. One can travel to over eighty countries, practically anywhere in the world.

Aside from formal learning, there is informal learning. This can be through books, mastering the computer and other modern devices, or working with another to learn a particular skill. Subjects that can be studied may include photography, nature, cooking, gardening, and any number of crafts.

Before I completed my higher education, I was sick of exams. When I finally ended my formal education, I vowed to continue learning, but to never take another exam. I learned of educational companies such as *The Great Courses,* whereby you can actually take courses taught by college professors from universities like Harvard, Stanford, and Princeton, all in the comfort of your own home with CDs, tapes, audio or DVD, without having to worry about cramming for exams. *The Great Courses* offers the subjects of fine arts, music, business, economics, science, mathematics, history, philosophy, religion and theology, literature, and language.

One of the best ways to continue to learn is by

reading. It has become clear to me that it is also a good exercise for the brain, which has a positive aspect as one grows older. It has been said that, "Reading is to the mind what exercise is to the body." Reading can range from ancient history to modern history, philosophy, scientific works, detective mysteries, biographies, novels, and a whole host of other subjects. Reading can also be one of the most enjoyable of hobbies. Just knowing that a treasured book is sitting at your bedside table can bring excitement and anticipation for the return home after a long day. It has been pointed out that book-lovers never go to bed alone. In addition to exercise for the brain, Sir Francis Bacon made the observation about books that, "Some books are to be tasted, others to be swallowed, and some few to be chewed and digested." Cicero commented on books as well. He said, "Other recreations do not belong to all seasons nor to all ages, nor to all places. These pursuits nourish our youth and delight our old age. They adorn our prosperity and give a refuge and a solace to our troubles. They charm us at home, and they are not in our way when we are abroad. They go to bed with us. They travel about with us. They accompany us as we escape into the country."

Travelling, such as on your own or through the hostel program, can be a form of learning, but it is not always possible to do. However, through books, you can still go places. For example, I always wanted to go to Australia, but, unfortunately, I never have and probably won't have the opportunity. But I don't feel short-changed for when I read *The Thorn Birds* by Colleen McCullough, not only had I been there through my reading, I learned of Australia's history, and I thoroughly enjoyed the stories of her characters through the generations. It is books like *The Thorn Birds* which can give you entertainment, educate you, and allow you to travel to foreign places in your mind. James Michener's book *Chesapeake* took me to Maryland, and after reading Michener's *Alaska*, I felt I had been there as well; *Sarum* by Edward Rutherfurd gave me an excellent understanding of English history and was quite enjoyable; and Tolstoy's *War and Peace* would tell me of Russia's history. These books are historical fiction and one of the best ways to learn and be entertained at the same time. While these books are very long books, I've learned to view each chapter as a short book and before long, I've finished the book.

I've been a reader off and on all of my life. But after I began my quest, I truly learned to love reading even more. I've certainly benefitted from it. Through my research and my reading of history, I visited ancient Sumeria at its peak, I trekked across the sands of Egypt during the times of the Pharaohs. I saw the rise of the Greek civilization and its ultimate demise. I watched while Rome rose from a small city-state on the Seven Hills to become the ruler of the known world. I crossed the English Channel with the Romans and witnessed how a small island became the British Empire upon which the sun never set. I wandered through the Dark Ages after the fall of Rome until the Renaissance finally took hold and brought the western world back into the "light" once again. I suffered through the Black Death as it ravaged mankind and its result, but which ultimately benefitted man by helping to free him from serfdom. I sailed with Columbus to the New World and with Magellan around the world. I was there when America was settled and witnessed the U.S.A. become a super power of the world. Through my research and my reading I met a cast of characters from ancient times until the present which have influenced my life.

Books can be the best of friends and keep you connected to the world. Dr. Charles Eliot points out that "Books are the quietest and most constant of friends; they are the most accessible and wisest of counselors, and the most patient of teachers." And that, "The pleasures of reading are, of course, in good part pleasure of the imagination; but they are just as natural and actual as pleasures of the senses, and are often more accessible and more lasting."

Moreover, Helen Keller, who was always learning, loved reading, and once remarked, "When I read the finest passages of the *Iliad,* I am conscious of a soul-sense that lifts me above the narrow, cramping circumstances of my life. My physical limitations are forgotten – my world lies upward, the length and the breadth and the sweep of the heavens are mine!" She went on to say, "In a word, literature is my Utopia. Here I am not disfranchised. No barrier of the senses shuts me out from the sweet, gracious discourse of my book-friends."

Reading as described by Ms. Keller doesn't just apply to works such as the *Iliad*, but it can apply to any books, depending on your interest. The enjoyment of a book can be an adventure in itself. Reading can be one of the best of companions, and as I pointed out, can take you to foreign lands, and you can even have the experience of living more than one life. Former Californian Senator and college professor S. I. Hayakawa once said, "It is not true we have only one life to live, if we can read, we can live as many as we wish." Gandhi speaks on this subject when he points out that, "Whoever has a taste for reading good books is able to bear loneliness in any place with great ease."

When it comes to reading, I don't know how many times through the years I have had people tell me that they do not have time to read. This contention is refuted by the author Louis L'Amour, who was known for his many western novels. He pointed out in his autobiography, *Education of a Wandering Man,* that reading is an easy exercise if one will only pursue it. He demonstrated that anyone can have plenty of time to read. L'Amour said he would read as many as twenty-five books a year while waiting in offices, such as the dentist, and on buses, trains, and planes. And all of us, especially as we get older, should have plenty of time waiting in doctors' offices and the like. He went on to point out that through reading you can learn something that can be with you your whole life long.

But, if you don't want to read, you can always listen. Many books are now available as audio books for rent or to buy. In fact, I have a friend who enjoys knitting, and while using her hands to knit, she listens to audio books.

Regardless of how you learn, whether through reading or otherwise, the basis behind learning is the satisfaction of curiosity. In other words, the desire to learn. I now realize that you must never lose that inquisitiveness for it is the "lure of wonder" and "the unfailing childlike appetite of what's next" as pointed out in Ullman's poem that keeps us young. This is all a part of the acquisition of knowledge, and according to the French Renaissance writer, Montaigne, "There is no desire more natural than the desire for knowledge." The people I studied who stayed young all of their lives were curious; they were interested in people; they stayed amazed at nature and the world in general; and how things work. They stayed excited about life and were interested in life and all of its aspects, never losing their curiosity or their desire for more knowledge.

One of the most curious people I studied was Bertrand Russell. He looked upon life as an adventure. "Isn't it wonderful," he once said, "to *find out* things?" Russell seemed to be interested in everything --- ethics, human knowledge, logic, mathematics, philosophy, science, religion, and politics. He was an avid reader of newspapers, serious non-fiction books, and devoured an average of one detective novel a day. Russell's quest for knowledge and his curiosity continued right up until his death at age ninety-seven.

The actor and t.v. star Steve Allen, former *Tonight Show* host who was married to the actress Jayne Meadows for over forty-five years, was so curious, always learning, and creative, that he wrote fifty-three books and composed over 4,000 songs in his seventy-eight years. Never growing old, Allen was writing his fifty-fourth book at the time of his death.

Among the life-long learners was Thomas Jefferson. His curiosity was such that his interests never seemed to be satisfied. Among other things, he was interested in music, chemistry, biology, architecture, farming, philosophy, law, and education. He would say, "There is not a sprig of grass that grows uninteresting to me." Comprised of thousands of books, Thomas Jefferson's library was so diverse and so vast that when the British burned the U. S. Library of Congress during the War of 1812, Jefferson's library was used to rebuild the library, which became the base of the Library of Congress that we have today.

Albert Einstein never stopped learning and was always curious. He once said, "People like you and me never grow old, we never cease to stand like curious children before the great mystery into which we were born." Curiosity was a part of Benjamin Franklin's whole being. He was interested in archeology, climate change, electricity, lightning rods, lead poisoning, stoves, canal boats, astronomy, phonetics, English grammar, other languages, population, smallpox, embalming, whirlwinds, swimming, geology, sunspots, magnetism, carriage wheels, evaporation, salt mines, coal, music, weather, using copper for roofs, insects, toads, glass-making, silkworms, the gulf-stream, politics, economics, health, eye glasses, and day-light savings time. His interests and curiosity would result in his inventing the Franklin stove, forming an academy which later became the University of Pennsylvania, forming a military company, forming the Union Fire Company of Philadelphia, and establishing a police force for the City of Philadelphia.

P. M. Roget, famous for his thesaurus, never stopped learning and satisfying his curiosity in his ninety years of life. His library included over 4,000 volumes dealing with math, engineering, medicine, science, literature, history, travel, philosophy, theology, politics, taxation, legislation, art, music, business, and even game books and joke books. Roget — tall, thin, clean-shaven, white-haired, normally dressed in black — was also known for his daily walks in London with his round-handled walking-stick. In addition to learning, he would work on and improve his thesaurus right up until his death.

The social and educational reformer, John Dewey, described what is meant by a curious mind: "The curious mind is constantly alert and exploring, seeking material for thought, as a vigorous and healthy body is on the *qui vive* for nutriment. Eagerness for experience, for new and varied contacts, is found where wonder is found." Russell, Allen, Jefferson, Franklin, and Roget all fit Dewey's description of the curious mind. And they all stayed young.

What is nice is that today, learning is easier than ever. Moreover, it can be so much more fun to learn. As Jefferson said, one needs to "keep pace" with the world; thus, you if you want to stay young, you need to jump on the bandwagon in this modern world of computers, I-Pads, I-Phones, and E-Readers. Many of my contemporaries have not done so, and they are missing out, not only on the present, but the future as well. These devices can bring the world to you; by "googling" almost any subject, you can get instant answers to satisfy your curiosity and to help you learn something. Information is truly at your fingertips. You can learn how to do almost anything, such as gardening, crafts, etc. You can even obtain information on volunteering. You can learn about law, such as wills and estates; in fact, all of my research today in my law practice is on the internet. Now you can even watch movies on these devices, and you can keep up with the news by the hour; you can get recipes if you like to cook; you can get medical information if you're concerned about your health. The list is endless as to the things that you can learn or discover through the computer and the internet, which will help keep you young. Although most of the people I studied lived before the internet, their minds were always open to new ideas, experiences, and learning — whether in music, reading, politics, or even food. A man once said, "One's education should never end until the last breath is taken."

CHAPTER 11

THE SIGNIFICANCE OF ATTITUDE

"To one man,
the world is barren, dull, and superficial;
to another,
rich, interesting, and full of meaning."
Schopenhauer

What General Douglas MacArthur and I both learned is that if you want to stay young, you must keep your aerials up. Thus, keep a positive attitude. A number of years ago, a good friend of mine learned that he had prostate cancer. The prognosis was not good; the cancer was such that he was told that he may only have months to live, and certainly not many years left on this earth. Rather than give up and surrender to the cancer, he went to MD Anderson Cancer Center in Texas. One of the first things he was told was that attitude was maybe just as important as any treatment that they could prescribe, and that if he maintained a positive attitude, it could only help in his treatment. From that day forth, with that advice and the support of his family, he never looked back and continuously maintained a positive attitude. Years later, he is still with us, going strong, and is cancer free.

Each one of us are the masters of our own lives; we can have a positive attitude or a negative attitude, regardless of what life deals us. This philosophy is not new. In fact, it was among the teachings of the ancient philosopher, Epictetus, who was born a slave in 50 A.D. During his childhood, he was crippled by his master; at the age of fifteen he was sent to Rome in chains and sold to another master; later expelled from Rome by the Emperor Domitian and forced to settle on the coast of Greece, where he would remain for the rest of his life, still in the status of a slave, but free to teach his philosophy. This philosophy developed by Epictetus allowed him to live in a contented manner and with a positive attitude throughout his life, even though he was lame and the lowest member of society. He would contend through his teachings that you are happy because you want to be happy, that you are sad when you want to be sad, and that attitudes are formed within yourself and cannot be affected by outside forces, unless you allow it.

One person who would discover the benefits of the philosophy of Epictetus and the rewards of maintaining a positive attitude was James Stockdale, a navy pilot during the Viet Nam War. Stockdale, prior to his deployment to the Far East to fly missions in Viet Nam, was given one of Epictetus' books by a professor while in graduate school. Stockdale would read and study Epictetus, not realizing that Epictetus' teachings would become one of the mainstays of his life. On September 9, 1965, Stockdale's plane was shot down over Viet Nam. He said that when he ejected from his airplane and was parachuting into enemy territory, he realized that he was leaving the world of technology and entering the world of Epictetus. Stockdale would be a prisoner of war in Hanoi for the next seven and one-half years. Tortured fifteen times, in solitary confinement for over four years and leg irons for two years, Stockdale said that it was the teachings of Epictetus that carried him through. He recalled that Epictetus taught that, "No one can harm you without your permission." Regardless of the punishment that Stockdale received to his body as a prisoner, he refused to allow it to affect his inner being. With this positive attitude, Stockdale found

141

peace within himself throughout his years of confinement, even under these extreme and adverse circumstances.

As Ullman points out, we can continue to be young all of our lives for it is "a state of mind". Even with the problems that aging may bring, one can still find contentment and happiness and reap the benefits of a good life by maintaining a positive attitude. Several years ago I was introduced to someone who reminded me of the importance of attitude. When we greeted each other, I observed a man who was slightly stooped and who was wearing a frown on his face. With my normal salutation, I inquired of his well-being. He replied that he was not in the best of health or spirits since he was an "old man". I quickly retorted that he did not look old to me, and then I asked his age. As he replied, he seemed to stoop even further and cast his face toward the ground as if he had aged even more after my question. "I am sixty years old," he stated. After hearing this revelation, I gleefully, with straightforward posture, answered, "you're not old, for I'm sixty-one." He seemed surprised by my acclamation, but within seconds he switched his story from his sufferings from old age and began chanting that his problems really stemmed from injuries that he received while serving in the military many years ago. As I viewed this man, I saw no missing limbs and noticed no other obvious physical impairments to substantiate his story. While doing so, I couldn't help but think of the many individuals I had encountered in my research who had suffered every type of physical and economic woe, and yet, they continued to smile and endure — finding joy in their lives, even under the worst of circumstances. It was obvious to me that this man was suffering from a case of misapplied attitude. Unfortunately, no matter how far I cared to delve into his so-called sufferings, he would obviously have another reason to convince me of his ills.

But how does one maintain a positive attitude? How do you keep your aerials up? I've learned that you have to work at it. "What you think, you become," said Gandhi. Thus, you have to think positive thoughts. Once I read that to keep positive thoughts, Pablo Casals, for eighty years, began his day by playing Bach's music to bring beauty into the beginning of each day and to remind himself of the pleasure of being alive.

As the dove is the symbol of peace and the cross the symbol of Christianity, Pablo Casals' symbol was his music — I call these inspirations. MacArthur used the poem *Youth* as his inspiration to remind him to stay young. As John Adams grew older, he drew his inspiration to stay young from the words of Cicero's essay *Cato Maior de Senectute.* "For as I like a young man in whom there is something of the old, so I like an old man in whom there is something of the young; and he who follows this maxim, in body will possibly be an old man but he will never be an old man in mind."

In a judge's office one day I saw on his wall a framed picture of a Christ-like image with the following words underneath: "I didn't say it would be easy, I said it would be worth it." It's no doubt that this judge who had to deal with the problems of others every day, and probably some of his own, drew inspiration from these words.

While in law school, I worked for a lady who always had a positive attitude. When quizzed as to how she maintained it, she replied that once a year, she and her husband would vacation in Missouri where she would sit by a lake, read and study Norman Vincent Peale's *The Power of Positive Thinking.* This was her inspiration. She said she had read it so many times that her underlining practically covered the whole book.

Russell Conwell, who fought for the Union Army as a Captain in the Civil War, would keep his sword above his bed throughout his life to always remind him of a resolution he had made to the memory of an extremely religious sixteen year old soldier, Johnny Ring, who had rescued Conwell's sword which had been lost in enemy territory, unfortunately, with Johnny Ring dying in the effort. To carry out his resolution, Conwell would become the minister at Grace Baptist Church in Philadelphia, Pennsylvania, serving until his death at age eighty-two. In addition to his ministry, he started a night school for young people to go to college who couldn't afford to go during the day. That night school became Temple University, which during his lifetime, educated over 100,000 students. In addition, he helped found the Good Samaritan Hospital in Philadelphia. Conwell was also known for his speech-making, of which his main speech was entitled "Acres of Diamonds", which helped thousands of people with their lives. On his 70th birthday, he gave the speech for the 5,000[th] time. The speech was given in every state in the union, and any monies he received for the speeches were given to needy students at the college that he had started. Drawing his inspiration from the sword, he kept his promise to Johnny by becoming a minister and helping young people. At his death, Conwell was buried with the sword.

Also I read of a woman who was continuously happy; when asked the secret of her happiness, she answered that she kept a book of her favorite quotes, prayers, and other up-lifting sayings. When she was inclined to fret, she would read a few pages to remind herself of what a happy, blessed woman she was. Of course, James Michener drew his inspiration from the old apple tree.

But, one of the most unusual but entertaining inspirations that I learned of was from my old neighbor friend who conversed with me from time to time across the fence. He told me of an elder friend of his that was so old that when he awoke in the mornings, he would open one eye and slowly look around to make sure where he was – whether in heaven or elsewhere. When it was clear that he was still here on earth, he would turn to his bedside table where he kept a *Playboy* magazine. He would then turn the pages to the centerfold and cast his eyes upon the human flesh to get his blood flowing — only then could he start his day.

Having mentors is also a type of inspiration. *Webster's* describes inspirations as things or people that inspire. I've learned that it can be important to find mentors to learn from and draw from their lives and apply it to your own. In his book, *Peace of Mind*, Joshua Liebman pointed out that, "Man loses his sense of direction when the compass of his soul is not magnetized by some great human star within the orbit of his experience." He further tells us that the ancient Greeks were educated on the principle of identification with Hellenic heroes; in other words, using as role models the heroes of the past to educate the young, which is education by example. For instance, *Plutarch's Lives,* which tells biographies of great men, has been used for hundreds of years as a model for teaching the young. Even Plutarch himself said it helped in his own life, "It was for the sake of others that I first commenced writing biographies; but I find myself proceeding and attaching myself to it for my own; the virtues of these great men serving me as a sort of looking-glass, in which I may see how to adjust and adorn my own life."

After leaving my home town and getting on with my life after my father quit the practice of law, I've had my own share of ups and downs. But I discovered that reading about others' lives could help me, as it did with Plutarch. In fact, Winston Churchill found mentors in men like Marlborough, Wellington, and Nelson, and Harry Truman found mentors in the lives of Andrew Johnson, James Madison, and Rutherford B. Hayes. Of course, mentors not only can be found in books, they can also be found in friends and others that you observe or share your life with.

In further answering the question, how does one maintain a positive attitude, I've also found that habits can play a major role. Habits can either be good or bad, negative or positive. The choice is up to you. If you were to eat a candy bar at 3:00 each afternoon for approximately one week, I promise you that thereafter, you will not have to look at your watch to know when it's 3:00; for at 3:00 — bing! — an alarm will go off telling you that it's time for your daily candy. This is how habits are created, regardless of their category. So to develop a good attitude, you need to develop good habits. For example, if you make it a point to smile as much as possible and speak to others in a positive manner, it will become a habit, and that habit, in turn, will make you feel better about your own life and being. Elizabeth Cady Stanton, the 19th century suffragist, said, "I never encourage sad moods." To keep a positive attitude, she never allowed bad moods to creep into her mind; and she would work at physical labor or practical thought to create happier thoughts. Harry Truman said, "I always try to be as pleasant as I can." In other words, to get an upbeat attitude, it needs to start with your own self. The White House reporter, Sarah McClendon, started each day with positive thoughts. "It has been a privilege to have lived this life. I can't wait to get out of bed each morning to start living more." Also, James Allen tells us "... beautiful thoughts of all kinds crystallize into habits of grace and kindness which solidify into genial and sunny circumstances." And Lester Maddox, former Governor of Georgia, kept upbeat with his positive way of thinking when he said, "It's great to be alive, a lot of folks aren't, you know."

Even in the face of death, the humorist Art Buchwald maintained a positive attitude. Buchwald, who wrote syndicated columns for newspapers, was told by doctors that he only had a few weeks to live because of kidney problems. He moved into a hospice and prepared for death. Even though he had reached this state of health, he kept writing his column. However, the unbelievable occurred in that he did not die as had been predicted by his doctors. Even though he remained ill which resulted in the loss of a leg, he never lost his humor or his love of life. In fact, during this period, he would write a book, *Too Soon to Say Goodbye,* and he even declared that, "I never realized dying was so much fun". Eventually, he would die, as all of us must, but he would maintain a positive attitude to the last.

Another way to keep a positive attitude is to count your blessings. For instance, our lives today are so much better than of yester-year, that we all need to rejoice. In 1769, you might travel a full day and only cover about thirty miles; whereas today, my normal drive to work and back home entails the same distance and is covered in less than an hour. Traveling from New York to Philadelphia in 1817 took three days; whereas today by car, only a few hours. In

1826, there were no airplanes, so if you went from New Orleans, Louisiana to Liverpool, England, it may take as many as sixty-four days at sea; and these were not necessarily "safe" days on the ocean, for one in six ships crossing the Atlantic was lost at sea.

In addition, today virtually every home has a telephone; in fact, with cell phones, almost every person has a telephone; but in the United States in 1900, only one home in thirteen had a telephone. And in 1904 in the United States, life expectancy was only forty years of age; more than ninety-five percent of all births took place at home; the average worker made only $200.00 - $400.00 per year; most women only washed their hair once a month and used borax or egg yolks for shampoo; crossword puzzles, canned beer, and iced tea had not yet been invented; only one in ten adults could read or write; only six percent had graduated from high school; only 144 miles of roads were paved; and there were only eight thousand cars on the road. Conveniences and blessings are all around us today – just look around and count them.

Furthermore, I've learned that if you want to maintain a positive attitude, don't dwell in the past. It is natural to cherish old memories, but to dwell on them can only bring melancholy. People who stay young look forward, not backward. Hildegarde, a famous Cabaret singer and dancer who performed for almost seventy years and was still performing in 1995, at the of age of eighty-nine, stated, "I rarely look back. That's the secret of staying young." And it was noted in the obituary of Richard Stanley Berry of Mendenhall, Mississippi who died in 2002 at the age of 104 that as an example of his life long optimistic spirit, Mr. Berry re-planted a tree farm when he was ninety, and harvested it when he was 100. The obituary went on to state that when his freezer quit at the age of ninety-seven, he bought a new one and even "took out an extended warranty policy".

James Michener, another who never dwelled in the past, said that he found even "in the ninth decade" of his life, that he was able to keep "remarkably viable" because he had remained alert to all things that happened around him and he was "always looking ahead to new challenges, never back to old victories." At age eighty-seven, George Burns said, "I look to the future because that's where I'm going to spend the rest of my life." He was so optimistic about the future, and not dwelling in the past, that he booked Caesars Palace for his 100th birthday, and remarked, "I can't die, I'm booked."

However, if your thoughts keep turning negative, there may be a need for a change in your life to get your thoughts back on the positive trail, such as changing your life in some fashion, like starting a new career or finding a new hobby. In this regard, in business, there is a principle that says that all products have a demand curve. If left alone, the product will pass into obscurity. But, the curve can be extended by changing the product or its appearance; thus, the detergent Tide, All New Tide, Tide with Color Brighteners, etc. I believe that every person is no different than the products of business. He or she must constantly renew themselves in some manner. So like the product, to stay young and to keep a positive attitude, one must continually work at changes or improvements of one's self. To ignore this could bring about old age before it is due. Thus, you are the product – renew, regenerate, reinvigorate — to do otherwise may bring about old age before its time.

There is nothing worse than an encounter with a person with a negative attitude. They can ruin your whole day. A friend of mine was speaking of a mutual friend having a bad day, but my friend chimed in, saying, "He wasn't having a bad day; he's having a bad life." To have a positive attitude, you must be an optimist. I've found an example in a book entitled *Life and Literature* which contains a collection of proverbs and sayings, one of which describes the difference between an optimist and a pessimist: "When it rains, the pessimist says: 'the rain is coming down in sheets; it makes me sad to think about the mud that will be in the streets. And all the crops and things washed out.' The optimist says: 'This rain will wash the dirt away, and leave the pavements nice and clean; I needn't use the hose today to keep the front yard looking green.'"

There should be no reason for one to ever have a negative attitude. Even though the Jazz legend Pete Fountain lost almost everything through bad business ventures, he kept a positive attitude. He said, "I can have a good time in a phone booth. Why be grumpy? I'm enjoying what I got left." Henry David Thoreau said, "If I were confined to a corner of a garret all my days, like a spider, the world would be just as large to me while I had my thoughts about me... However mean your life is, meet it and live it... The fault finder will find faults even in paradise. Love your life, poor as it is. The setting sun is reflected from the windows of the alms-house as brightly as from the rich man's abode..." And the thoughts of Thoreau can be magnified by the poem of John Kendrick Bangs:

"If there's no sun I still can have the moon,
If there's no moon, the stars my needs suffice;
or if these fail, I have my evening lamp,
or, lampless, there's my trusty tallow dip.
And, if the dip goes out, my couch remains,
where I may sleep and dream there's light again!"

We must never forget as Ullman tells us in his poem, that "in the center of your heart and my heart" there is that "wireless station", and when the "aerials" of that station "are down" then your spirit will be covered with "snows of cynicism". So I have learned that to keep that positive attitude you need to make sure that your inner self always receives those "messages of beauty, hope, cheer..."

Ullman's poem, as it had done for MacArthur and the Japanese people, gave me the tools to work with in order to keep young. But, I felt there were still a few more concerns that needed to be addressed to have a complete picture of what I sought through my quest. So leaving no stones unturned, I moved on to other subjects.

CHAPTER 12

STAYING YOUNG — EVEN WITH PROBLEMS

"We must learn to endure what we cannot avoid."
Montaigne

"Into each life some rain must fall," says the poet, Longfellow. Problems come in many ways; financial, physical, mental, or just "plain old change". Abigail Adams said it this way: "No one is without difficulties, whether in high or low life, and every person knows best where their own shoe pinches." Voltaire was stronger in his declaration when he said, "Life is a struggle to the last." I've learned that it's not that problems won't come, for they will; it's how we deal with them as they appear that counts. Benjamin Franklin tells us the best way to deal with problems when he wrote to his sister, Jane Mecom, "It sometimes is cloudy, it rains, it hails; again 'tis clear and pleasant, and the sun shines on us. Take one thing with another, and the world is a pretty good sort of world, and 'tis our duty to make the best of it and be thankful."

Among the woes we may face, financial problems are at the top of the list for many. Millions of Americans are struggling to live on merely a social security check today. In recent years, the United States has been mired in a financial crisis, resulting in people losing much of their savings and the equity in their homes. The country is in debt up to Uncle Sam's chin, and Social Security, Medicare, and Medicaid appear to be going broke. Things look dire; but we must remember the words of the Roman Emperor Marcus Aurelius, "Nothing happens to any man which he is not framed by nature to bear."

Even during the era of Marcus Aurelius, Rome had its financial woes, and the world has had its financial problems from time to time throughout history. We've experienced the bursting of the real estate and credit bubbles, but there have been bubbles in the past as well. For example, the Tulip Bubble of 1637 and the South Sea Bubble of 1720, both resulting in false wealth being created, but only to come crashing down causing financial ruin for many. Furthermore, the "muckraker" Ida Tarbell described in her autobiography a short history of financial problems just during her lifetime. She said she was born in the year of a major panic in 1857; thereafter, in 1866, there was a worldwide depression, and major panics in 1873, 1877, 1897, and 1917. My point is that financial problems have existed throughout history, and the panics were some of that rain that had to fall, but, like Franklin said, the sun did shine again. But how have people in the past dealt with these financial problems? I turned my research to this question.

I always thought "misery loves company" was a negative statement, but, as I progressed through my project, I found people could endure their problems much better if they knew others had suffered as well, particularly if those others overcame their problems, or learned how to endure them. For example, if you are suffering from financial problems, it may make you feel better to know that Mark Twain did also. In his sixties, he lost most of his fortune in a panic in 1893, but, he didn't give up, and instead, to recoup his losses, began a worldwide speaking tour, at an age when he had hoped to be retired. John and Abigail Adams lost most of their savings when they were in their sixties when a banking house failed in 1802, but they carried on. Thomas Jefferson, always in debt, particularly in his latter years, continuously borrowed money (even from his family), and had to borrow $8,000 in order to leave Washington at the end of his presidency; he died in debt owing over $100,000, which would probably be well over a million dollars today. But he never let the financial problems that he suffered prohibit him from living a long, full, and happy life.

Like Jefferson, Susan B. Anthony was in debt much of her life, yet she continued her pursuit with vigor for the rights of women and did not allow her debt problems to deter her mission in life. The painter John James Audubon had severe debt problems a good portion of his life and was even put in jail at one point for his debts, but this did not deter him from his painting. Bertrand Russell was terminated from his teaching position at the age of seventy, leaving him with a wife and three young children to support; but instead of giving up, he turned to his writings, never looked back, and successfully overcame his problems. Also the famous trial lawyer, Clarence Darrow, at age seventy-three, was almost penniless because of the stock market crash in 1929. But, rather than give in, he continued trying cases until he was eighty. Another example was James Madison, who after leaving the White House, became a full-time farmer, had to live on borrowed money in his last years. All of these individuals picked themselves up, dusted themselves off, and continued to look to the future and lived as best as they could, maintaining a positive attitude, rather than succumbing to their woes. Thus, anyone can follow their examples and do the same.

Money is important, but not that important; financial concerns should not affect one's outlook on life or keep one from living a full life and staying young throughout their life. I believe the proper attitude towards money needs to be like that of the French artist Henri Matisse, who stated, "I began an artist's life very poor, and I'm not afraid to be poor again." He knew that no matter what his financial situation might be, he could continue to find happiness and satisfaction in life through his art.

Financial problems aren't the only hardship that some of us may encounter. For example, physical problems will probably beset most of us if we live long enough. Even modern medicine will not be able to cure or correct every problem. But the important thing I've learned is that the people who stayed young found ways to live full, happy, and productive lives even though they were faced with physical adversities.

Andrew Jackson, from age fifty-four until his death at seventy-eight, was in pain almost every day. He had two bullets lodged in his body: one bullet in his chest from a duel with Charles Dickinson which was so near his heart that it could not be removed, and a second bullet from a shoot-out with the Benton brothers. Both bullet wounds caused Jackson to suffer from abscesses, fevers, spasms of coughing, and even hemorrhages throughout his life. In addition to these bullets, he suffered from dysentery and malaria, and his health slowly declined as he grew older. However, Jackson would still run for the presidency of the United States, serving in that office with its many duties, maintaining a positive outlook on life, regardless of the pain and health problems he suffered.

Physical problems also beset the pianist Arthur Rubinstein in his latter years. His eyesight failed, and he was in constant pain; yet, at age ninety, he was dictating his memoirs, playing records four to five hours a day, and listening to young pianists who came to play for him. Rubinstein, even under these circumstances, stated that he was living the happiest years of his life.

Likewise, Henri Matisse, at age seventy-one, suffered from intestinal cancer, which resulted in an operation and hospitalization for almost three months. The operation was considered a success, but it would severely change Matisse's life in that he was often bedridden, and had to wear an iron belt which made it impossible to stand for long periods. But he viewed the operation as giving him a "second life", for which he rejoiced. This "second life" began in 1941 and lasted until his death thirteen years later. Despite these problems, he would continue to have amazing vitality throughout the remainder of his life, saying, "Endowed with this additional life, I could do as I wished. I could create what I had struggled for all these years."

Like Matisse, the writer, Reynolds Price, whose writings have been compared to William Faulkner, had his physical problems as well. He developed a malignant tumor at fifty which wrapped around his spinal column, resulting in operations, radiation treatments, and ultimately being paralyzed from the waist down. Yet his most prolific writing would begin after this tragedy with him claiming that writing actually became easier for him than before, and like Matisse, he viewed the remainder of his life after his paralyzation as a whole new life. Matisse and Price contended that their physical problems actually gave them a second chance in life, for which they were thankful. They found good out of bad. They truly turned lemons into lemonade.

Others, because of their physical problems, have even found that it was an opportunity to start a whole new career for their life. Dorothea Dix, who, because of her health problems, as I mentioned, quit teaching and found her life's mission in helping the mentally ill. Grandma Moses began painting as a result of severe arthritis in her hands which prevented her from embroidering because she could no longer hold the needle. What she did learn, though, was that she could hold a paintbrush with her gnarled fingers; thus, at seventy-six she began painting and continued until her death at age 101. Today her paintings hang in nine museums throughout the United States, Vienna, and Paris.

Problems come in various ways; they can be financial or physical as we have discussed, but for many, there are mental problems, such as worry. I've learned that the word "worry" comes from the old Saxon language and is derived from the sound caused by the choking or strangling of an animal when seized by the throat by another animal. In the early years when language was being created, if a person heard the sound of an animal in distress, that person may have feared he might be next. Thus, the sound represented "worry". However, most worry is for naught, just like when Chicken Little in the old English folktale cried, "Oh, Help! The sky is falling!" Of course, the sky wasn't falling; it was merely an acorn that had fallen on Chicken Little's head, but the worrying by Chicken Little was as bad as if the sky was truly falling. It has been said that worrying is broken down in the following manner: 40% of things worried about never happen; 30% of things worried over are in the past which can't be changed; 12% are needless health worries; 10% are petty miscellaneous worries; and only 8% are truly legitimate worries. Dr. Charles Eliot said it this way: "We must remember that the misfortunes hardest to bear are those which never come." As you can see, worrying is mainly a waste of time and it can even make you sick. To stay young, you must not worry; it can affect your health, your happiness, your attitude, and maybe even your longevity. Thus, as Ullman tells us in his poem *Youth*, "Worry, fear, self-distrust, bows the heart and turns the spirit back to dust."

But even if we don't worry, we may still have problems; but like aging, problems are part of living. If we live long enough, one of those problems that will come into our lives will be sorrow, for we will lose loved ones along the way. Unfortunately, there is no true cure for sorrow, only time may heal. As Jean de La Fontaine, the French poet of the 17th century, tell us, "On the wings of time grief flies away." There may be no cure for sorrow and grief; however, there may be ways to deal with it. Mark Twain had to deal with sorrow after his wife, Livy, died. He suffered greatly but found that work was the best way for him to deal with his grief. He said, "This has been the saddest year I have ever known. If it were not that work brings forgetfulness, life would be intolerable." Also, Gordon B. Hinckley, who was serving as President of The Church of Jesus Christ of Latter Day Saints when his wife of sixty-seven years died, addressed the problem of grief when he said, "The best thing you can do is just keep busy, keep working hard, so you're not dwelling on it all of the time. Work is the best antidote for sorrow." Like Twain and Hinckley, when Konrad Adenauer's wife, Emma, died, he wrote, "Work is a drug to alleviate my suffering."

The ancient philosopher, Epictetus, said you should deal with grief in this manner: "Never say about anything, 'I have lost it,' but only, 'I have given it back. Is your child dead? It has been given back. Is your wife dead? She has been returned. ... So long as God gives it to you take care of it as something not your own..." But to stay young, you cannot let sorrow and grief cause you to "give up enthusiasm", and you must keep receiving messages of "hope and courage".

Even change can be a problem for some. I am reminded of a lady who moved from her home into an independent living facility. Her new quarters consisted of a wonderful two bedroom apartment adorned with her favorite beautiful furniture, paintings, and the like, along with a kitchenette and windows which overlooked a small lake. The facility provided three meals a day in a restaurant-like setting, as well as transportation for medical and grocery shopping. The facility also had a small library, a computer for use by the occupants, a small beauty parlor, and even provided entertainment. All this sounds pretty good to me, but when asked about her activities, this lady would answer that she only sat and stared at the four walls, for she missed her old home. Before long, the four walls began to close in on her, and she found herself miserably unhappy. There is no doubt in my mind that had she absorbed herself in activities that were available to her in the independent living facility and pursued interests which would have kept her mind off of herself, she would have found a means to happiness, rather than a means to misery, thus creating her own problems. I have found we have to remember that all of life is a period of adjustments, and sometimes we just have to acquiesce, but rather than fret, we need to make the best of the circumstances. An old Chinese proverb says that "a wise man adapts himself to circumstances, as water shapes itself to the vessel that contains it."

Problems will come in into your life; it's not whether, but when, and what kind. However, no matter what your problems may be, you shouldn't quit. Betty Hutton, who starred in movies such as "Annie Get your Gun" and "The Greatest Show on Earth", would become one of the top singers and actresses of Hollywood, earning as much as

$150,000 a week by 1950, and would amass a wealth of ten million dollars. By 1965, her stardom had faded, and her problems began: she succumbed to depression, took pills, drank alcohol to excess, and contemplated suicide. Within ten years, she was broke and working as a cook and housekeeper at a Roman Catholic Church in Rhode Island. But she didn't quit, and she began to work at getting her life back on track once again. She attempted to re-emerge into acting and singing but did not succeed. Nevertheless, she didn't give up. Instead, even though she was over sixty, she sought a whole new life and purpose. She enrolled in college earning a bachelors degree and afterwards, obtained a masters degree in psychology. By her late sixties, she was teaching at Emerson College in Boston, Massachusetts. She died at the age of eighty-six knowing that fame and money didn't necessarily mean success, and that problems could be overcome.

Among those who didn't quit, even though he had lost the respect of his fellow man, was Richard Nixon. I was no fan of his, particularly after Watergate, but I have to admire him for his tenacity in building back some of the respect that he had once known. Here's a man who in his own words stated, "No one had ever been so high and fallen so low." At his highest point, he was in charge of the richest and most powerful nation on earth; but, by the time the dust had settled from his foolish mistakes, he would have to resign from the office of the presidency. He not only brought dishonor upon himself, but embarrassment to his family and those who had supported him. He would be barred from the practice of law in California and New York and became so hated by many that he could not even live in certain parts of the country because of the ill will and disgust that he had wrought upon himself. But Nixon did not give up. At sixty-one years of age, he studied, wrote, and built a new reputation for himself as an elder statesman. He would write his memoirs and published them at the age of sixty-five. Later, he would write seven books regarding world affairs. Before he died at age eighty-one, he would once again be sought out by world leaders for his advice. I remember how the politicians clamored to be at his funeral on April 27, 1994 at the Nixon Library in Yorba Linda, California. Over 4,000 attended the services, including every living president and their first ladies, and the then-President Bill Clinton. Eulogies were given by former President Gerald Ford and Senator Robert Dole. Dole would quote Nixon when he spoke of failure, "... you should never be discouraged by failure. Failure can be sad, but the greatest sadness is not to try and fail, but to fail to try. In the end what matters is that you have always lived life to the hilt."

Regardless of what problems may beset you, try using the words of Frank L. Stanton's poem for inspiration:

"Keep a-Goin"

If you strike a thorn or rose,
Keep a goin'!
If it hails or if it snows,
Keep a-goin'!

'Taint no use to sit and' whine
When the fish ain't on your line;
Bait your hook an' keep a-tryin'-
Keep a-goin'!

161

When the weather kills your crop,
Keep a-goin'!
Though 'tis work to reach the top,
Keep a-goin'!

S'pose you're out o' ev'ry dime,
Gittin' broke ain't any crime;
Tell the world you're feelin' prime-
Keep a-goin'!

When it looks like all is up,
Keep a-goin'!
Drain the sweetness from the cup,
Keep a-goin'!

See the wild birds on the wing,
Hear the bells that sweetly ring,
When you feel like surgin', sing-
Keep a-goin'!

CHAPTER 13

TIME AND THE LURE OF RETIREMENT

"What a wonderful life that would be,
in which there had been
no lost moments,
no lost thoughts,
no lost good deeds."

Russell Conwell

So many people have all the elements of youth while they are working, raising a family, are in good health, and chronologically young. But when the time comes that these cease to exist, people sometimes go into a downward spiral resulting in a loss of positive attitude and even a reason for living, for they no longer have a purpose; they have lost "the lure of wonder, the unfailing child-like appetite of what's next, and the joy of the game of living." They no longer have goals, and their life becomes a ship without a rudder, and they become old.

Even though they are adrift with no chartered course, the time left in their life continues on and can continue for many more years. When the Social Security Administration was founded in 1935, someone age sixty-five could expect to live only eleven more years. According to present life expectancy tables, if you are sixty-five, you have an average life expectancy of approximately eighteen more years. Thus, one-quarter of your life may still be left to live if you are in your sixties. In fact, it is projected that life expectancy by the year 2050, could be eighty-six years for males and ninety-two years for females. You may live as long as "Old Tom Parr". So what are you going to do with that time?

Regardless of your age, the sand continues to pass through the hourglass; therefore, that time which is left allotted to you should not be wasted. I now keep an hourglass on my desk as a reminder for this purpose. One thing for sure that I have learned is that people who stayed young didn't squander their time. Benjamin Franklin certainly recognized the value of time. In his *Poor Richard's Almanac*, he printed the proverb, "Dost thou love life? Then do not squander time, for that is the stuff life is made of." Seneca, the Roman Stoic philosopher, pointed out that life is long enough if we invest in it carefully. Seneca went on to say that we should welcome the later years of our lives for they are full of pleasure if one knows how to use that time.

Unfortunately, we cannot plan our lives to their finality since we do not know when our final moment will come; therefore, we must plan according to the life expectancy tables. But, since there are no guarantees, we need to make sure that each day is lived as if it is our last. Nevertheless, that time can be wasted, or it can be used wisely in a manner which benefits humanity, our families, and ourselves. However, the earth will keep revolving around the sun, the clock will keep on ticking, and the time will pass, whether we use it wisely or not. But remember, life is a gift, and it should be treasured, savored, and not squandered. Seneca said, "Why are you idle? If you do not grasp the day, it flies away." He speaks again, "No one can restore years, no one can give you back to yourself."

Marcus Aurelius tells us that, "Time is like a river of fleeting events, and its current is strong; as soon as something comes into sight, it is swept past us, and something else takes its place, and that too will be swept away." What's funny is that time seems to pick up speed as we get older and passes by ever so quickly. However, the clock ticks at the same pace whether you are twenty or eighty. You still have the same hours in a day that you have always had. But people who stayed young didn't fritter the hours away. Emily Dickinson reminds us, "That it will never come again is what makes life so sweet." And Charles Darwin spoke of time also when he told us that a man who dares to waste time has not discovered the value of life. Along these lines, I was shocked to learn that on average, older people watch as much as forty-three hours of television per week. This seems like a crime to me when there is so much that can be done to enrich their lives or help the lives of others.

It has become clear to me that the best life is the complete life; we get out of life what we put into it. Emerson tells us "to finish the moment, to find the journey's end in every step of the road, to live the greatest number of good hours, is wisdom."

In one's latter part of life, the question of retirement usually arises. Being In my seventies, hardly a day goes by that someone doesn't ask, "Aren't you retired yet?" When are you going to retire?" What immediately pops into my head is, "retire to what?" I once read that if you retire, make sure that you retire *to* something, not just *from* something. Bob Hope, when asked about retirement, answered, "Me? Retire? If I retired, I'd be surrounded by about nine psychiatrists. I'm not retiring until they carry me away." He never did retire. I believe that the view of retirement of most people is what the English statesman, Arthur James Balfour, said: "Give me my books, my golf clubs and my leisure, and I would ask for nothing more. My ideal in life is to read a lot, write a little, play plenty of golf and have nothing to worry about..." Unfortunately, it usually is not like this.

I'm a little like Bob Hope in that it is not my desire to retire. Slow down, maybe, or even change professions, but retire, no. If I did retire, or at least slow down, what would I do with that time? This question sent me searching, and what I found was that retiring in the traditional sense is not a trend that is continuing today. I've learned that many older workers are working past the usual retirement age, not because they necessarily have to, but because they want to. In fact, the number of workers sixty-five and older who are choosing to keep working has been on the rise for more than twenty years. Besides most U.S. retirees admit they miss purposeful work activity, and three/fourths said they would like some type of paying job. Unfortunately, so many people dream of retirement rather than stay immersed in their daily activities and career, only to find out that retirement is not what they had dreamed of, and as a result, they inadvertently grow old. You can only play so much golf.

I recall a few years back when my car was being repaired that I had to use a service vehicle for transportation to my office. I struck up a conversation with the lady who was driving me, and she related a story regarding retirement. She said both she and her husband retired at the same time from their respective jobs, and within a few months, they had done everything that was on their "retirement list". Their daily mornings thereafter started with drinking a cup of coffee at the kitchen table and then asking each other what they were going to do that day. She told me "boredom had set in" and they had nothing to do. Finally, one day over the morning coffee, her husband asked her "What are you going to do today?", and she replied, "I'm going to find a job!" And she did. She began driving the service vehicle as her new job. Within a matter of days, her husband said, "Do you think they would have a job for me at that company?" She replied, "I'll check and see." Sure enough, the company hired him as well to be a substitute driver for her. After a while, they even became a team whereby they were able to drive to various car dealerships throughout the country to pick up vehicles needed for sale, considering the trips as mini-vacations. They were happy to be back in the mainstream of life.

Unfortunately, idleness so many times can become the center of one's life upon retirement. Benjamin Franklin in his autobiography made this observation regarding idleness: "This gave me occasion to observe, that, when men are employ'd, they are best content'd; for on the days they worked they were good-natur'd and cheerful, and, with the consciousness of having done a good day's work, they spent the evening jollily; but on our idle days they were mutinous and quarrelsome, finding fault with their pork, the bread, etc., and in continual ill-humor, which put me in mind of a sea-captain, whose rule it was to keep his men constantly at work; and, when his mate once told him that they had done every thing, and there was nothing further to employ them about, 'Oh,' says he, 'Make them scour the anchor.'"

Moreover, when I considered work versus retirement, I began to realize that retirement may even be detrimental to your life and to your health. I once knew a lady who was an excellent primary school teacher for many years. She had a gift for working with children and could create, narrate, and write children's stories. She could have taught for as long as she wanted; she was in fairly good health, but when she reached that magic age of possible retirement, she realized that time might be running out and she had so much she wanted to do that could not be done if she continued to teach. Like so many, she began to long for retirement. She dreamed that she would work in her flower beds, write her autobiography, and write those children's stories that she created so well. Who knows? She might publish a book of children's stories and get rich! She would take time to visit friends, play bridge, and do all the other activities that she dreamed of that could only be done in retirement. Her life would be full. She would have purpose and direction. She had a sufficient income from her retirement and social security, and she even had a part-time job selling books to supplement her income, so it was clear that she would not have to live by the structured means that teaching required. Retirement day finally arrived. What a relief! How wonderful life would now be! She would now be able to fulfill her dreams, and not live by the clock or under the supervision of others.

After settling into her retired life, she sat down to write her memoir. It was fun, but not quite as easy as she thought, so after writing for a few days, she started putting off that project — it could wait until another day. After all, she was retired. It was summer and the weather was hot, so she also put off working in the flower beds — it also could wait until another day. After all, she was retired. Also, selling books meant bothering people about something they may not want, so that could be started later also, but not right now. After all, she was retired. Instead, she would think more on the type of children's books she would write, and when she was ready to write, she could write. After all, she was retired! She had the rest of her life to get her projects going.

Before long, she started watching television to fill up some of the hours in the day, and she discovered that having a drink every day made the day fun, especially if there was a football game to watch and her favorite team was playing. As time went by, all of her goals and dreams that she had upon retirement just slowly drifted away and were replaced by a day-long whiskey buzz. She no longer had purpose or direction in her life. In my opinion, she had grown old; and, as Samuel Ulman pointed out in his poem, she had deserted her "ideals". Her days continued like this, until she was finally put into a nursing home because she could no longer function on her own.

Another person that comes to mind regarding time and retirement was an elderly gentleman I knew. Like our lady, he retired so he could have the days to do with as he wished. He had grown up on a farm, then became successful in the city. I would see him from time to time when he would visit his son's business establishment. One morning as I walked into their offices he was relating a tale that he was writing in his autobiography for his family and friends. He stated that the mule or horse that he was plowing with had been giving him trouble, the dirt was hard, and the weather was hot. At a certain point in time he said he plowed that last row, unhitched the animal, and made the decision that farm life was no longer for him. This would begin the next chapter in his life whereby he moved to the city. His story lines that he related were wonderful, humorous, and kept me thoroughly entertained. I knew his book when finished would do the same. I told him I would like to have a copy of his book when finished, and he agreed. Thereafter, I would ask him how the book was coming, but he would only say that he hadn't gotten back to writing it. Soon, months went by, and then years, and finally, his death. No book. I would have loved to have read that book if only it had been completed, and I know his family would have too. The point here is that this is typical with the so-called "retired" — they dream and set goals, but then they lose direction and drift through their latter years with good intentions, but do not follow through. They violate Benjamin Franklin's maxim – *they wasted time.*

These scenarios repeat themselves everyday. I once read, "If you want to ruin someone's life, give him too much free time." That lady and that gentleman were given all the time in the world and thought they had purpose and direction in their lives when they retired, but they did not. They stopped listening to that inner self which would have given them the means by which to carry out their ideals, goals, or dreams. They failed to keep their "aerials" up. Instead, they languished in idleness and just grew old. Sir Walter Scott said that when we break a day by idleness in the morning, the rest of the hours lose their importance in our eyes. A man once said that laziness grows on people; it begins in cobwebs, and ends in iron chains.

I'm not advocating a sixteen hour work day for the retired; but, I am suggesting that certain principles must be followed if you want success in your remaining years. Unfortunately, most of us associate the word "working" with "formal employment". But, Webster's Dictionary makes it clear that working is not necessarily formal employment but is any "bodily" or "mental effort exerted to do or make something." In other words, "purposeful activity." Thus, when Grandma Moses was painting at age 100, she was working, for she was involved in a purposeful activity. When Hulda Crooks was hiking and conquering mountains, her activities were setting an example for other elders that strenuous physical activities could still be performed no matter how old you are; this was a bodily effort on her part, and thus, she was working. Also when Samuel Ullman was writing his poem "Youth", he was working, and that work would help change the world.

"The less I have to do, the less time I have to do it in." This is one of the problems with so-called "retirement"; one's life seems to shrink to the point that they are doing nothing which falls into the category of work — meaning they are doing nothing by way of purposeful activity, improving themselves, or serving mankind. In fact, it has been written that, "A man's worst difficulties begin when he is able to do as he likes." Retire from your present occupation if you must, but don't mistakenly retire from life. Jack Valenti, long-term President of the Motion Picture Association of America, addressed this situation when he said, "Retirement for me is a synonym for decay." Work can only be beneficial for you, whereas idleness or misdirection will only be a recipe for deterioration. Likewise, work can also be a form of exercising the brain, thus, good for your mental health. It has been shown that older adults who work at stimulating or complex jobs perform better in tests of cognitive function than peers of the same age who do not do such work. Auto leader, Lee Iacocca, said, "Don't retire. Your mind will atrophy..." Swiss philosopher Carl Hilty, who lived during the late 19th and early 20th centuries, in his *Essays on the Meaning of Life*, felt so strongly about working that he believed "that regular work, especially as one grows older, is the best preservative both of physical and intellectual health." He also pointed out that "idleness is infinitely more wearisome than work..." wasting time, especially when it comes to retirement, Hilty tells us, "Most of the wrecks of human life are caused by having either no work, or too little work, or uncongenial work; and the human heart, which is so easily agitated, never beats more peacefully than in the natural activity of vigorous, yet satisfying, work." Konrad Adenauer, whom I mentioned earlier, was a disciple of Hilty, and perhaps Hilty's teachings inspired Adenauer to build a new Germany.

So if you retire from your employment, you need to find a new purpose, set new goals and carry them out, or old age will slip up on you when you should have many good years left. When President John Quincy Adams was defeated for re-election to the presidency, rather than stop working, he chose to seek a lower office instead of retiring. He ran for and was elected to the House of Representatives at the age of sixty-four and held that office until his death seventeen years later. Also, George Franklin Edmunds, who was a member of the U.S. Senate, left Congress in his sixties after serving for twenty-five years, but rather than retire, went on to become a noted expert on Constitutional Law. Susan B. Anthony made it clear that she never wanted to retire when she said, "I don't want to die just as long as I can work. The minute I can't I want to go. I find the older I get the greater power I have to help the world."

Work can also help you through the rough spots of this life, and may be good food for your mental health as well. Charles Darwin, who had many health issues, said, "I only forget myself when I'm at work." Albert Einstein also spoke of work: "As long as I am able to work, I must not and will not complain, because work is the only thing that gives substance to life." And Voltaire points out that if one keeps working, there may be much to gain when he said, "The further I advance in age, the more I find work necessary. It becomes in the long run the greatest of pleasures." Voltaire went on to say, "Work keeps us from three great evils, boredom, vice, and need." And William von Humboldt said, "Work, according to my feeling, is as

172

much of a necessity to man as eating and sleeping."

What's amazing to me is that so many people, especially when retired, say there is nothing to do. There is plenty for one to do. For example, one can garden, which is certainly a purposeful activity, thus, work. It also is good for your health and is something that you can do all of your life. In fact, I recently read of a retired coach who at eighty-two was maintaining a garden of peas, onions, potatoes, corn, tomatoes, radishes, and squash. In addition to the exercise that he got from his garden, he attributed his good health to the fresh vegetables that he harvested and ate each year.

Another way to keep from wasting time is by volunteering your time. Over sixty million Americans volunteered in 2009. There are many ways to volunteer – through schools, churches, hospitals, fire departments, food banks, museums, zoos, and other institutions. There are organizations such as The Gleaners, The Gideons, United Way, The Salvation Army, March of Dimes, and the like who are always seeking volunteers. If you don't wish to volunteer your time with an institution, you can take it upon yourself to volunteer your time for your neighborhood. Maybe pick up trash and garbage on the block in which you live. In fact, I once read about an elderly lady who wanted to have a nice, clean neighborhood, so she would sweep the sidewalks on her block. Also, I read about a gentleman who watched his neighborhood deteriorate through the years; however, he decided to do something about it. So instead of relaxing in retirement, he started a neighborhood restoration organization to reclaim and restore the homes. Mahatma Gandhi once said, "You must live for others and not only for yourselves. Idleness is demoralizing."

Writing is another means of work which may keep you from wasting time. Writing can create a family memoir which can be treasured after you're gone, or it can be possibly financially rewarding. Frank McCourt, an English teacher for many years, retired to the writing craft, and wrote *Angela's Ashes,* a story of his youth. His book became a best-seller, won the Pulitzer Prize, and made him a lot of money. Likewise, Mireille Marokvia published two memoirs in her eighties and nineties which described her childhood in a French village during the occupation by Nazi Germany during World War II. And writing is an activity which has no age limits. In fact, Galen Clark wrote three books on the California trees and Yosemite Park — all after he was ninety years old, and Millie Benson, author of *Nancy Drew* mysteries was still writing at the age of ninety-six. She said, "Writing is a way of life for me. It's like getting up and having breakfast."

You can even turn a hobby into a business; you can teach or further your education so you can teach; you can take up an art or craft; you can learn something new such as the computer which may lead you to work; you can even go into politics. The list is endless, and a book could be written in itself on the various ways to achieve and find success and rewards in your later years. The important thing to remember is that you cannot sit around and do nothing, nor can you make plans and then drift from those plans, or you'll find yourself old before your time. You must find work, thus purposeful activity, and go about fulfilling it. Remember always what Thomas Carlyle once said, "Blessed is he who has found his work; let him ask no other blessedness. He has a work, a life purpose; he has found it! Labor is life..."

Just recently I saw a doctor friend of mine who was

not aware that I was writing this book. As we chatted, he proclaimed, "I have discovered the secret of the fountain of youth." Of course, my ears perked up immediately, and I said, "What is it?" He replied, "Work." Thereafter, he went on to state that he had noticed that people who continued to work throughout their lives in a slow but steady pace, such as small business owners, just continued on and on, and then one day, they just dropped over dead. But they lived long lives and stayed young until their deaths.

Unfortunately, so many people associate work with too much energy to be expended during their latter years. But Andres Segovia, who kept an unbelievable schedule of work going until his death at age 94, pointed out, "I will have an eternity to rest." In the *Book of Wise Sayings Largely from Eastern Sources* you will find the following: "The every-day cares and duties which men call drudgery are the weights and counterpoises of the clock of Time, giving its pendulum a true vibration, and its hands a regular motion; and when they cease to hang upon the wheels, the pendulum no longer sways, the hands no longer move, the clock stands still."

So if you are drawn to the rocking chair, you should remember the words of an unknown author who describes the importance of work:

If you are rich, work,
If you are burdened
with seemingly unfair responsibilities, work,
If you are happy, continue to work;
Idleness gives room for doubts and fears.
If sorrow overwhelms you
and loved ones seem not true, work,
If disappointments come, work.

When dreams are shattered
and hopes seem dead, work,
Work as if your life were in peril;
It really is.
No matter what ails you, work,
Work faithfully and work with faith.
Work is the greatest material remedy available.
Work will cure both mental and physical afflictions.

CHAPTER 14

REMEMBER — YOU'RE NEVER TOO OLD

"If wrinkles must be written upon our brows,
let them not be written upon the heart.
The spirit should not grow old."
James A. Garfield

Over three thousand people were packed into the Dorothy Chandler Pavilion in Los Angeles, California. There were young shapely starlets everywhere. All the beautiful people were there. Rosy cheeks, red lips, supple knees, and cleavage were abound. As the stars paraded down the red carpet, the flashes from the cameras were like fireworks on the 4th of July. More than forty million people were tuned in from all over the world on March 26, 1990 to watch the 62nd Annual Academy Awards. As Gregory Peck opened the envelope, silent prayers and wishes were made, and fingers were crossed. But the night would not belong to those with supple knees, but, instead to an eighty year old lady, who still had the "freshness of the deep springs of life", who continued to seek "adventure over the love of ease", who never grew old by deserting her ideals, and who continued to "catch the waves of optimism." In his deep, resonating voice, Gregory Peck announced, "And the Oscar goes to Jessica Tandy." The audience would be ecstatic. There would be a standing ovation for Ms. Tandy, the winner of the Best Actress award for her role in "Driving Miss Daisy", becoming the oldest to ever receive the award and be revered by the world for her accomplishment.

Acting since she was sixteen, Jessica Tandy would not reach the pinnacle of her success until that night when her dreams had been fulfilled. In her own words, she had reached "cloud nine". Even though she was eighty, she had not grown old for she had never given up her enthusiasm. Nor did she retire afterwards. That same year when she learned she had ovarian cancer, she continued to act and work pursuing her purpose until her death. Jessica Tandy taught me that you're never too old.; her feat would give me new energy for my own quest.

Accordingly, I continued to search for others who have also proven that you're never too old. I found them in different professions, with different skills, and in all walks of life. I was amazed at the number of people I found performing feats, learning, working, competing, and creating in their latter years as if they were half their age long after so-called retirement for most.

Among those was George Abbot, winner of six Tony awards, who wrote and directed such plays as "Pajama Game", "A Funny Thing Happened on the Way to the Forum", and "Damn Yankees", wrote two of his plays between rounds of golf at the age of ninety-eight and was still writing on his 100th birthday; at age 102, he was the co-director of an off-Broadway play "Frankie" and would keep working right up until his death at age 107.

In the field of law, I remembered my friend, Billy Nichols, who was still a full-time deputy sheriff with the Hinds County, Mississippi Sheriff's Department at the age of eighty-six. I learned of Albert R. Alexander, who served as a Probate Judge for Clinton County, Missouri until the age of 105.

Unfortunately, so many people only picture in their minds those over seventy as sitting in a rocking chair or walking with a cane; but, twenty-nine American World War II veterans, whose average age was seventy-two, would certainly dispel this image. In the year 2000, these brave and adventurous men made a dangerous trip to fulfill a dream by steering a WWII ship across the Atlantic Ocean in order to set up a floating museum in Mobile, Alabama. Even though they were warned of the dangers of crossing the Atlantic in an antiquated ship, they chose "adventure over the love of ease" which, as Ullman pointed out, "often exists in a man of sixty more than a boy of twenty". Although the ship was cranky and old, they succeeded in their mission, proving that the nay-sayers were wrong, and they were able to celebrate an event that they and their families will cherish forever.

Those men chose adventure; others have chosen learning to prove that you're never too old to learn and that youth is "a matter of the will". Eugenie Garside went back to school at Cape Cod High to earn her high school diploma, receiving it at age ninety-eight after crossing the stage on her walker to a standing ovation. And I found Doris Travis, who interestingly was the last of the Ziegfeld Girls, went back to school and earned her high school diploma in her seventies, and then continued her education receiving her college degree at the age of eighty-eight; but she didn't stop there – she continued working on her masters degree. But the old dancing spirit from the Ziegfeld days stayed with her, for she was still dancing at the age of 104.

One of the most creative that I discovered proving that you're never too old was John Suta, who so wanted to learn to play a musical instrument that he became a member of a middle-school band at the age of seventy-six so he could learn to play the French horn.

Even the game of checkers found its way into the "never too old" category. I learned that Asa A. Long, in 1922 at the age of eighteen, became the youngest U. S. National Champion at checkers; but, he would win once again, at age seventy-nine, in 1984, making him the oldest champion at checkers as well.

Moreover, volunteering appears to have no age limits, and it probably shouldn't. For instance, Dr. C. L. Austin, at the age of eighty-seven, made a 166-mile trip each Monday to volunteer his medical services at a clinic on the Mississippi Gulf Coast after Hurricane Katrina. Likewise, Dr. John Burson proved that one can volunteer and serve his country at the same time, when at the age of seventy-six, he was on his fourth tour of duty with the Army Reserves overseas; his tours included two in Iraq and two in Afghanistan.

As my research continued, I found many musicians who were also enjoying the "fountain of youth" such as Dave Brubeck, the Jazz pianist, who was still performing and playing his piano in concerts at the age of ninety. At age 100, Lionel Ferbos was playing his trumpet at the Palm Court Jazz Café in New Orleans, Louisiana. And Peggy Gilbert formed "The Dixie Belles", a Dixieland Band of older women, when she was sixty-nine, continuing to perform in the band until she was ninety-three. And the guitarist Les Paul won two Grammy awards for an album that he recorded at age ninety.

Actors, like musicians, seem to stay young forever. Rex Harrison was still performing at age eighty-two; Helen Hayes at eighty-eight; Katharine Hepburn, who won four Academy Awards as Best Actress (three after the age of sixty) was still acting at the age of eighty-seven; Hal

Holbrook, at eighty-five was still performing his one-man show "Mark Twain". And Kitty Carlisle Hart was still singing and performing on a cruise ship in her 90th year, and was still performing on the stage at ninety-six, declaring, "...I'm lovin' it."

Adventure and courage should not only be for the younger years. As Ullman pointed out, one can still have adventure over the love of ease at any age. For instance, Leni Riefenstahl continued to take on new challenges and learn new things all of her one hundred years. Likewise, Sir John Ross, the English explorer, was exploring the arctic ocean at the age of seventy-six in the 1800's. And even former President George H. W. Bush, in his eighties, was jumping out of airplanes to celebrate his birthdays. William Ivy Baldwin crossed the South Boulder Canyon in Colorado on a 320 foot-wire over a 125-foot drop on his 82nd birthday, and Fred Mack celebrated his 100th birthday by skydiving; his first sky-dive wasn't until he was ninety-five. Peggy McAlpine, a British grandmother, who, at the age of 100, became the world's oldest paraglider. Chuck Yeager was breaking the sound barrier at the age of seventy-nine in a F-15 Eagle jet plane. Keizo Miura skied down the glacier Mont Blanc Valle Blanche in the French Alps on his 99th birthday. And David Clark circumnavigated the globe alone in a boat at age seventy-seven, saying "I wanted to send a message that dreams are achievable."

Those who continued to work, regardless of their age, were Caspar Weinberger, even though he was on kidney dialysis, at the age of eighty-eight, was traveling the world and writing a regular column for *Forbes* magazine. Bill Watts of Ridgeland, Mississippi, confined to a wheelchair, was still working by sharpening tools and welding jobs at age eighty. Additionally, John W. Smith of

Blue Mountain, Mississippi, at the age of ninety had a yard service whereby he worked six days a week, keeping up forty-nine yards and two cemeteries, sometimes in 98 degree heat. Fannye Mae Gibbons, at age eighty-six was still operating her beauty salon in Jackson, Mississippi, after fifty-six years. (Pulitzer Prize Winner Eudora Welty was one of her regular customers). And Harold Fisher was still working as an architect at the age of 100, saying, "Work is my first love. It has kept me alive."

When it comes to sports, the young have nothing over the old. Ulrich Inderbinen took up competitive skiing in the Alps at the age of eighty, and in his nineties, he regularly climbed peaks of more than 13,000 feet; it has been estimated that Inderbinen had stood on the summit of the Matterhorn at least 375 times. Dimitrion Yordanidis, at the age of ninety-eight, ran a marathon in only seven hours and thirty-three minutes. Sam Gadless of Boca Raton, Florida, who did not take up running until his seventies, entered his first marathon at the age of eighty-five, and at ninety-one, was the oldest entrant in the 1998 New York City Marathon. Norman Vaughan, a dog-sled racer, completed the Iditarod Dog Sled Race thirteen times, having made his first run when he was almost seventy and his final Iditarod at age eighty-four. In addition, Vaughan celebrated his 89th birthday by climbing the South Pole's Mt. Vaughan, which was named for him when he explored the South Pole with Admiral Richard E. Byrd.

You might think that most older people have never mastered the internet, but, this was dispelled when I found some old geeks there also: Maria Amelia Lopez, who at ninety-five, began blogging, covering a range of topics from Basque separatists to Iran's nuclear ambitions; and Ivy Bean of Great Britain, at 104, had 27,000 twitter followers and at least 5,000 friends on "Facebook".

Because creativity continues throughout our lives, one is never too old to create. Antonio Stradivari created his two most famous violins in his nineties, and Elliott Carter was composing music and was still in his prime at age 100. Joe Grant, an artist who created Disney characters in the movies, "Dumbo", "Snow White", "Pinocchio", and "The Lion King", was working at his drawing board in his home studio when he died at ninety-six.

Among those who stayed young were Henry Boehm, an itinerant Methodist preacher for seventy-five years, travelling over 100,000 miles on horseback. At the time of his death at 100, he was the oldest Methodist preacher in America. And Arthur Lessac, vocal coach of Michael Douglas, Faye Dunaway, Martin Sheen, and others, at 101, was emeritus professor of theater at State University of New York, and only a month before his death, was teaching at a university in Croatia. Activists such as Doris Haddock, with false teeth, two hearing aids, and severe arthritis, walked across America (3,055 miles) to call attention to campaign finance reform at the age of eighty-nine, completing her walk at the age of ninety.

Others who inspired me were Carolyn Kelly, who at age eighty-two, stripped off her clothes and dove into a pond in Shreveport, Louisiana, saving the life of an eighty-three year old. Edward Payson Weston, in 1909, at the age of seventy, walked across the continental U.S. in 104 days and crossed back over the next year in 76 days. Floyd "Creeky" Creekmore, at ninety-five, was named the "Oldest Performing Clown in the World". Nora Hardwick, a British woman, at 102, posed topless for a calendar as "Miss

November" to raise money for her local football team.

I realize that all of us can't be a Jessica Tandy or a Leni Riefenstahl, or like some of the others I've described, but what I have learned is that none of us should sit around and look at four walls or fritter our lives away, nipping on a bottle of wine all day. If nothing else, we can be the best grandparent in the world. Surely each one of us can find something that we can be passionate about and pursue, which will be good for us, our families, or our fellow men. No matter how old you are, change and growth are not beyond you. *Old dogs can learn new tricks.*

It is clear to me that those who stay young have goals, continue to take risks, and pursue their dreams and find excitement and pleasure in their lives, no matter how old they are.

You're never too old
to plan and dream;
You're never too old
to eat ice cream.

You're never too old
to enjoy a good meal;
You're never too old
to ride a ferris wheel.

You're never too old
to buy a toy;
You're never too old
to find some joy.

You're never too old
to smell a rose;
You're never too old
to write some prose.

You're never too old
to take a trip;
You're never too old
to skinny dip.

You're never too old
to skip and run;
You're never too old
to just have fun.

You're never too old
to give a hug;
You're never too old
to cut a rug.

You're never too old
to try and win;
You're never too old
to start again.

You're never too old
to make a wish;
You're never too old
to catch a fish.

You're never too old
to take a chance;
You're never too old
to find romance.

You're never too old
to wear a smile;
You're never too old
to kid awhile.

You're never too old
to hold a hand;
You're never too old
to play in the sand.

You're never too old
to plant a tree;
You're never too old
to sail on the sea.

You're never too old
to steal a kiss;
You're never too old
to try and miss.

You're never too old
to make new friends;
You're never too old
to stay 'til the end.

You're never too old
to read a book;
You're never too old
to stop and look.

You're never too old
to laugh and cry;
You're never too old
to sail and fly.

You're never too old
to help a friend;
You're never too old
to receive and send.

You're never too old
to learn something knew;
You're never too old
to comfort a few.

You're never too old
to watch a play;
You're never too old
to enjoy each day.

So when you feel age is
creeping up on your back,
Just read this poem
to get you back on track.

For no matter what age
you may be,
You must always be ready to agree,
You're never too old.

CHAPTER 15

LAST THOUGHTS

"The man, who has no place for death in his philosophy,
has not learned to live.
The lesson of death is life."

Anonymous

My quest is over, but my life is not. I am now many years older than my father was when he spoke those seven words of despair to me. When I think over these last years and the life that I've lived, I realize now what all my father missed by giving up on life. I hope I will have many more years left, but I intend to enjoy myself and not be a prune – even if it shortens my life. I don't plan on applying for a disability sticker just so I can get the closest parking spot, for I figure if I can get in a car and drive, then I should be able to walk to the store. Besides, I probably need the exercise. No face lifts for me, no testosterone treatments. Let nature take its course with my body, but, I'll stay young in mind. And when my time comes, I will be ready. My bags are packed.

When I think of happiness, I'll remember Helen Keller, who, though blind and deaf, still enjoyed all of the beauty and the pleasures that life had to offer. I will try to always be absorbed in things besides myself as Jefferson did; I will remember that avarice is a disease of the old, and if I want to stay young, I will not succumb to it; and I will try to live by the old English proverb: *Forego, forget, forgive, Then happy you shall live.*

When I wake up and feel like "what's the use?", I

will climb out of bed to embrace the day, for I will think of John Wesley climbing on his horse in sleet and snow with his Bible in hand to continue to carry out his purpose. I will try to emulate Justice Holmes and continue to improve my mind. I will recall old Ben Franklin, who could be considered the youngest man at the Constitutional Convention, because he never stopped learning and his curiosity was never satisfied.

I'll continue to remind myself of Somerset Maugham's promise that old age has its pleasures, though different from the pleasures of youth. I'll continue to marvel at the strides of modern medicine in hopes that it will give more quality to my life as I age. I will periodically read the words of Samuel Ullman so as to remind me that "youth is not a time of life; it is a state of mind."

I will remember that if James Stockdale can survive for seven and a half years of imprisonment without "throwing in the towel" by remembering the teachings of a man who lived thousands of years ago, I, too, should be able to tolerate anything and keep a positive attitude. If I have physical or financial problems, I will recall Henri Matisse being thankful for his second life, and not afraid to be poor again. I will never retire in the traditional sense for I have learned that the love of ease can be a recipe for disaster. Nor will I waste time. And if I start something, I will finish it. Also, whenever I begin to feel old, I will picture Jessica Tandy receiving her Oscar, and I will strive to keep my "aerials up".

When I'm lying on my deathbed, I want to think of all the things I did during my life, and not think of regrets for the things I didn't do. I plan to continue reading many more books because I can learn something and enjoy them as well. I will play my music from the fifties and reminiscence, but I will remember that I need to always look forward and not back; thus, I will try to find new artists of today, for I want to stay in tune with today's world, as well as enjoy my past.

I've learned growing old — just like staying young — is a choice that each one of us can make. I am choosing to stay young. Also, I will remember that my mountain climbing lady, Hulda Crooks, stressed that as we grow older, we have a responsibility to show young people that life is worth living right up until the last for the youth need to see that we enjoy life, and that life is worth living at any age.

When I think of the future, and how long I may live, I will remember a gentleman in my hometown who was a small businessman, who, as time went by, became somewhat famous for his longevity. The last time I saw him, he was staring at 100. He was immaculately dressed in a crisp summer suit with a colorful flower in his lapel. It was at a restaurant known for its Sunday lunch, particularly for its tomato aspic, tea biscuits, and fried chicken. A table had been reserved for him as a special guest, and as he sat down, he had a big smile on his face, greeting all those around him. But before having his meal served, he first ordered an extra dry martini. While the voices and the stirring of iced tea glasses resonated throughout the room, he lifted his glass, gave a slight salute, and took his first sip. He was celebrating life. This is youth.

Keep your aerials up!